Tenderfoot Trail

Tenderfoot Trail

Greenhorns in the Cariboo

OLIVE SPENCER LOGGINS

Sono Nis Press
Winlaw, British Columbia

Copyright © 1983 by Olive Spencer Loggins
Interior illustrations © 1983 by Sonja Maans

Third printing, 2014

LIBRARY AND ARCHIVES CANADA CATALOGUING IN PUBLICATION

Loggins, Olive Spencer, 1900–1989
     Tenderfoot trail

ISBN 978-0-919203-44-0

     1. Loggins, Olive Spencer, 1900–1989   2. Frontier and
pioneer life—British Columbia—Deka Lake Region.   3. Pioneers—
British Columbia—Biography.   4. Deka Lake Region (B.C.)—
History.   I. Title.

FC3845.D.44L64   971..1'2   C83-091116-2
F1089.D44L64

Sono Nis Press most gratefully acknowledges support for our
publishing program provided by the Government of Canada through
the Canada Book Fund and the Canada Council for the Arts, and by the
Province of British Columbia through the British Columbia Arts Council
and the Book Publishing Tax Credit, Ministry of Provincial Revenue.

Interior illustrations by Sonja Maans
Cover design by Jim Brennan
Front and back cover photo of landscape by Rod Currie

Published by
Sono Nis Press
Box 160
Winlaw, BC V0G 2J0
1-800-370-5228

books@sononis.com
www.sononis.com

The Canada Council | Le Conseil des Arts
for the Arts | du Canada

I dedicate this book to the memory of my husband, Arthur James Spencer, without whose courage and determination our pioneering venture would never have taken place. He had always loved the great outdoors, preferring the northwoods to any crowded city. I often watched him as he followed with his eyes and with his heart, the flight of the Canada Wild Geese. I was prompted to write this sonnet which fits his mood so well.

WILD GEESE FLY

Our ears are tuned to catch their lilting cry
Gay spring has come, we watch with eager face
For that far shadow flung like finest lace
Upon the southern sky. The wild geese fly!
Strong-pinioned birds in close drawn units high
Flying boldly yet with infinite grace,
Their trooping flight we watch through tractless space,
Darkly etched and squadron-like along the sky.
We cannot follow to that lonely land
These other city-prisoned folks like me,
But we can vision on that northern strand
Canada's wild geese growing strong and free,
Though we are bound by customs' drab demands
Like them, unfettered, we could wish to be.

Contents

CHAPTER 1   The Cariboo Calls / 9

CHAPTER 2   Journey to the Cariboo / 17

CHAPTER 3   Isch-ka-bibble Country / 26

CHAPTER 4   We Learn How to Fish Through the Ice / 36

CHAPTER 5   New Year's Eve Party / 44

CHAPTER 6   We Buy Our First Team / 54

CHAPTER 7   Blizzard Brings a Visitor / 63

CHAPTER 8   One Woman Rodeo / 72

CHAPTER 9   I Visit Our Pre-emption / 78

CHAPTER 10   Indian Neighbours Become Friends / 84

CHAPTER 11   Visit to the Lazy J Ranch / 94

CHAPTER 12   Home on Dragonfly Lake / 102

CHAPTER 13   Arthur Saddlebreaks a Mustang / 111

CHAPTER 14   Danger Dodges Us as the Ice Breaks Up / 117

CHAPTER 15   Spring Comes to Dragonfly / 124

CHAPTER 16   Living and Learning in the Northwoods / 133

CHAPTER 17   Danger Comes Calling / 144

CHAPTER 18   Roping a Bull Moose / 153

CHAPTER 19   Our Cabin / 163

CHAPTER 1

The Cariboo Calls

THE GREAT DEPRESSION will never be forgotten by those who lived through it. British Columbia suffered as did the other provinces, perhaps more because thousands of unfortunate unemployed people found it easier to sleep on a damp park bench than to freeze to death on the Prairies or in eastern Canada.

In B.C., there were no jobs and men without a cent in their pockets had to queue up in lines at the soup kitchens run by the Salvation Army, the Shriners, Oddfellows and others, besides every church denomination, in order to receive at least one meal a day. These were the times before welfare and unemployment insurance. The situation looked hopeless and morale was never lower.

In 1926 my husband and I were living in Vancouver. We had saved our wages before we married and had built a little grey bungalow in the city. The depression upset our expectations for the future; life could obviously not go on as before. We were expecting our first child in three months. The economic climate was dreadful and I worried about how to pay the upcoming hospital expenses and how to manage afterwards. Our parents were in the same position as we were and unable to help financially.

The B.C. government had a plan, however, which was to roll back the clouds of the depression and, for us, reveal a silver lining. The government plan was to offer pre-emptions of land in a stipulated area of B.C. whereby settlers could improve upon one hundred and sixty acres by residing on the land for ten months of every year for five years, during which time they had to build a house and a barn and put up fencing. Land was to be cleared of stumps and dense brush, and prepared for planting crops. Usually these crops

9

were for feeding cattle. The plan called for energetic and willing settlers who would forgo the city conveniences in return for free land, hard work and prospects for a good future.

To my husband Arthur, the government offer seemed a wish come true. He burst into the house one gloomy afternoon after a long day of useless job hunting. But this time he was grinning happily. He grabbed me in his arms, waltzed me around the room and said, "There is a Shangri-la after all, it's not just a myth. There's an answer to our dreams, wait while I tell you all about it." He then told me of the pre-emption plan.

Arthur was not without experience in farming as he had worked for his uncles on large prairie farms in Saskatchewan and had handled large teams with harrows and ploughs. He was also proficient with a rifle; he had been a cadet in his younger days and won several cups for target shooting. He explained that this would be wild country where the pre-emptions were offered but that all his previous experience would stand him in good stead.

I needed some convincing and quietly weighed the pros against the cons. Here I was raised in a city and used to city conveniences. Though my mother had insisted on all her daughters learning how to cook (this included bread and making butter), I had never ridden on horses, knew nothing of guns and, on top of all this and more, I would soon have a newborn baby to care for. Arthur had mentioned that there were no doctors in the area and the nearest hospital was over eighty miles away. The project seemed very hazardous to me and I told my husband that it seemed a rather risky thing to attempt.

The happy look went out of his face, making me at once feel guilty, and it hurt me to see him so dejected. I remembered my marriage promises and cast caution to the winds, knowing at the same time that our present situation was tenuous and promised nothing. "Cheer up, my dear. We'll go. How soon can you file your claim?" Arthur was immediately up in the clouds again and said he had met a man who had already filed his claim and wanted to know if Arthur knew anyone with an old but reliable truck for sale. The man planned to drive up to his claim, taking his wife, three children and some household possessions along.

Arthur did know some men in the used car business and took this man to see some available trucks. He had considerable knowledge about the workings of truck engines and helped choose one which seemed to please the man. Arthur's new acquaintance confessed that he had heard the Cariboo road was very rugged and even dangerous in places. Indeed it was; certainly a far cry from today's Cariboo Highway, paved and wide. In 1927 there were places so worn from erosion that two vehicles could not pass safely. If two cars met, one or the other driver was forced to back up until a wide enough spot appeared to let each car pass. In any case, Arthur had already decided to get up to the Cariboo and scout out the land for a suitable pre-emption. He offered to do half the driving for this settler in return for a free ride up into the Cariboo. The proposal was accepted and arrangements made.

The next important step was to inform our parents of our new plans. Neither of us were prepared for the indignation that we roused. My father put his arms around me and said, grimly, "We wouldn't think of letting our daughter go up into such wild country. You've heard there are grizzlies and wolves and other predators up there, haven't you, Arthur? You wouldn't stand a chance. And you say there are no doctors or hospitals or police protection nearby. It's unthinkable, that's all."

Arthur's parents were equally upset by our decision; his mother could not appreciate the fact that we were young and healthy and ambitious enough to trade the unknown for the unpleasant present city life. "There are no people up there and I can't bear it for you to take our first grandchild so far away. We may never see any of you again." Then she burst into tears and we finally left, feeling like the basest criminals. But as far as we were concerned the die was cast. While I arranged to go on living at home, trying to find a buyer for our bungalow and preparing for the new baby's arrival, Arthur would join the Jordans (whose truck he was to help drive) and start off on the trip to find a suitable pre-emption.

With so many unemployed, selling a house was next to impossible, yet we needed the money to buy necessities for our new home. It wasn't until a week before my baby was born that an old school friend called to see me. She was excited to hear about our plans and told me she was to be married shortly. She looked about our cosy little house and said, wistfully, "What we'd give to be able to buy your house, Olive, but even with Ted and I both working we haven't enough saved up to buy."

I thought that my friend's wishes might be the answer to our problems so I asked her, "Perhaps you could arrange to pay $800 down payment with the balance monthly like rent?" Alice was astonished at the low figure, but I reassured her and asked her to bring Ted to see it. When Ted saw the house he was immediately happy with the idea and we made the deal then and there. Now I waited for the baby's arrival and for Arthur to come home so that we could complete our arrangements.

Our baby arrived before Arthur did. He was born on October 14th, and when I saw the tiny baby I proposed to take north, so far from urban conveniences, I had several attacks of worry. Then I admonished myself sternly. After all, we were not the first pioneers to go into the Cariboo and, within the family, our baby's great-grandparents had left Ireland, crossed the Atlantic and then traversed the prairies in covered wagons. On my side of the family, my ancestors had forfeited luxury, and in one case wealth, to leave England and travel to Canada and the United States. There have always been pioneers and my son was to be yet another. So, worries in perspective, it was a proud mother who greeted Arthur on his return from the Cariboo. He duly admired his son and we chose the name Roland for him.

I had had qualms about starting our move before the spring came. I knew that winter in the high plateau country we were heading for often boasted temperatures of 50 to 60 degrees below zero Centigrade. Despite the tasks that faced us before we could make a start, Arthur had no such qualms. He went into positive raptures about the beauty of the country, forests, lakes, valleys of wild hay, and what he called "a real cattleman's dream." Then he said, "I ran into a piece of luck up in Williams Lake. I met a rancher, Roy Charlton by name, and we got quite friendly." Roy Charlton had said he was happy to hear of more people coming to settle in the Cariboo. He had a ranch on Deka Lake about 25 miles east of 100 Mile House and ran a herd of cattle and a string of horses. Apparently, when he met Arthur, he was looking for a man with some experience who would go into his ranch and stay over the winter to feed and water the cattle while he took his wife to Vancouver for an operation. Arthur had offered his services, explaining that he would have a wife and child with him. Roy Charlton was delighted. "So we settled that you and I go into Roy's place and stay three months," said Arthur.

The location on Deka Lake was not too far from our own pre-emption on Dragonfly Lake. Arthur would be able to haul the things he would need when he built our own log cabin, and still come back to the Deka Lake cabin each evening.

Now that Arthur had arranged a temporary home for us at the Charlton ranch house we must choose the necessary articles and equipment we would need when we built our own log cabin. Our purchases would be shipped to Lone Butte. This deserted sounding place was the railroad station on the Pacific Great Eastern Railway, the place closest to the very unpopulated section of the province where we were to pre-empt our 160 acres of land. From the station, our household goods would have to be hauled by a team of horses and sleighs to Deka Lake.

To clear brush and cut down trees for building our own log house, Arthur had to purchase tools such as a crosscut saw, machete, axes, peaveys and a crowbar, besides other carpentry equipment. I had to buy housekeeping equipment. Utensils totally different from anything I had been used to, such as water pails, a wash boiler, a large wash tub that would have to double as a bathtub and stove irons. We needed a good wood-burning stove and bowls and pans for bread making. The electrical appliances I was used to would be left behind and we would be taking coal-oil lamps and lanterns with us. Other than our bed and Roland's crib, we would take no furniture. Arthur had decided to construct chairs and a table from trees he would cut on our own land. Ours was to be true pioneer living.

Given our funds, there was just one place to deal and that was a second-hand store; there were any number to choose from. We went into one. I looked at the list in my hand and then at the jumble of old assorted merchandise in the shop and suffered more inward qualms. I saw wash tubs, pails and sad-irons. The latter I could remember using as a child in one of the homes we rented that did not have electricity. To use one, the iron was heated on top of a wood- or coal-burning stove. Then, carefully wiping off the bottom of the hot surface, one applied it to the garment that was to be ironed. Quite often, in my case at least, a black smear would appear on the otherwise spotless material and ruin the whole task. Then one had to wash and go through the whole performance again, a most dispiriting job.

"Lady, you are interested in these old irons, perhaps? They make a very fine door-stop. Very fine, very funny, eh?" said the small shop proprietor as he smiled with studied humour. "Not funny at all!" I snapped. "I'll take four, but not to use as door-stops."

I vowed to myself that there would be little ironing done in my home on the range! Then I stopped dead in my tracks. If there is such a thing as love at first sight, then I had suddenly fallen in love with Kitchen Queen. There she stood, majestic in her beauty, her lines temporarily hidden in a jumble of miscellaneous objects which are always to be found in profusion in any second-hand store. She was imposingly large, crowned with a roomy warming oven, upon which her name was suitably engraved. But she combined utility with her grand manner, having on one side a large water tank which I knew would be invaluable for heating water for the baby's bath and doing laundry. Her oven was capacious, just the thing for roasting all those venison and moosemeat joints which Arthur had promised would be the mainstay of our meals. "Come and look, dear. I've found exactly the right cook stove to take with us to our new home. It's got simply everything!" My voice conveyed my enthusiasm because Arthur came over at once. He looked and turned thumbs down on my discovery. He quickly estimated weight and bulk and said firmly, "But that huge thing must weigh a ton! We couldn't possibly freight that thing all the way to Dragonfly Lake. You apparently have no idea of how little we can eventually take."

He actually called Kitchen Queen "that thing" and I was angry. So far he had been getting everything he wanted, but here was one place where I would assert myself. I answered as reasonably as I could, "We've simply got to have an efficient cook stove in that climate no matter what else we may have to do without. If the temperature drops to below 60 degrees, as you've been telling me, this stove may be the only thing that would prevent us from freezing to death. Then there's Roland, he's got to be kept warm no matter what you say." As soon as the proprietor heard the word baby he ranged himself on my side. Waving his hands imploringly, he positively entreated my spouse to buy Kitchen Queen. "The little lady is right, mister. Nothing is too good for your baby son, especially so when you are taking him to such a cold climate." Arthur stood his ground for at least a minute, then said, "You have never seen the kind of terrain this monster of a stove will have to be hauled over to get it to our future home." But the salesman and I were solidly behind a hot stove for a cold house. Arthur finally bought it and the shopkeeper, overjoyed at being able to sell the antiquated piece of steel and iron at a good price, generously threw in for nothing a shabby Quebec heater. Shabby or not, that heater was destined to do its full share of keeping the Cariboo cold at bay.

After purchasing numerous articles in that shop we went further and, a few doors away, Arthur discovered his own piece of treasure. Emerging from a pawn shop and carrying a rifle, he sounded pleased. "Say, this is a real piece of luck. I got it for peanuts, you might say. Some poor fellow down on his luck must surely have been broke; put this gun in hock and never had the price to get it back. It's a dandy and that's one thing a man has to have in game country, a reliable rifle. We'll never lack for meat, at any rate."

We wrote to the Charltons at Deka Lake and confirmed and thanked them for their kind offer. We planned to leave Vancouver, putting our belongings on the barge to Squamish, on November 20th. Our parents were very upset at our leaving but we told them that it was really not that remote—just a one day's train ride from Vancouver, a matter of three hundred and fifty miles. They promised to write often and my father said he would send the newspapers regularly so that we could remind ourselves that we still existed in this world. I felt a little sad at the prospect of cutting myself off from civilization; the pleasures of moving picture shows and the odd stage play. But I had to admit that there had been none of these since our pocketbooks had been so depleted during the long period of unemployment.

Finally we said our last good-byes and boarded the small passenger and freight ship which plied the waters of Howe Sound between Vancouver and Squamish. The Indian spelling for Squamish was Sku-whom-ish and it meant "The Place of Stormy Waters," but on the day we reached there, rain was teeming down and the sea was a dull grey, leaden and utterly cowed by the torrents. The small town nestled at the foot of high coast mountains and peered out at ships that sailed to the timbered wharf of the tiny port.

Squamish was the end of steel for the Pacific Great Eastern Railway. This line was built over seemingly impossible terrain, against almost insurmountable obstacles, at great cost and with almost superhuman perseverance. It was, even to my non-technical understanding, a positive marvel of railroad engineering. However, at that time, it bore the unenviable stigma of being considered a "white elephant" by the residents of British Columbia.

We got to Squamish and we were on our way.

CHAPTER 2

Journey to the Cariboo

THE LOCOMOTIVE had the distinction of being one of the oldest models extant and had probably been donated to the P.G.E. Railway by executives of some more prosperous line. It puffed and snorted into place at the head of a baggage car, one solitary antique coach and a medley of freight cars and flats. We stood and watched Kitchen Queen and our other belongings loaded into a freight car. Before long the conductor called "All Aboard," so we climbed onto the coach platform and bade farewell to the coast.

Traffic going into the Cariboo country on November 20, 1927 was not heavy, consisting of ourselves and one travelling salesman on his way to Quesnel which was the northern end of steel for the railway line. The train was scheduled to arrive at Lone Butte at 2 a.m. the next day, so we settled down for a long ride.

The decor of this coach would have gladdened the heart of any son of old Ireland. It was the most vivid emerald green, made of a velvet-like plush material which would have appealed, I think, to a hungry cow. I was able to add a distinctive contrast later by hanging up a washing to dry in the heat of the coach.

Arthur had told me that after our arrival at Lone Butte we should have more than thirty miles to travel by sleigh and it was probably my last chance to wash things for the baby until we arrived at Deka Lake. With the kind permission of the salesman who said he had children and knew what it was like, I asked the conductor if he could improvise a clothesline for me. He very obligingly did this, stringing the line the full length of the coach. I made good use of the hot and cold running water in the ladies' washroom, sadly reflecting that this would be my last opportunity to enjoy such facilities for a long, long time.

Having attended to laundry duties I was able to stare out of the train windows at the most breath-takingly beautiful scenery I had ever seen. Rugged blue and grey-toned mountains pushed their shoulders into the clouds, their heads hidden by clouds. Evergreen trees, fir, spruce, hemlock and cypress clothed these slopes, with sudden glimpses of white cottonwoods still spangled with golden summer leaves, like coins that no one had gathered, on the lower parts of the mountain slopes. Far below the right-of-way of the railroad, beneath steep and rocky canyons, I caught glimpses of the surging Cheakamus River, hurling itself through narrow gorges towards the sea.

I marvelled aloud at the ingenuity and ability of the engineers who had built this. Without the modern work-saving machines available today, they had worked against Nature in her most stubborn mood to provide access to the untouched wealth of the province's interior and permit the opening up of wonderful ranch lands.

The locomotive threaded its perilous way along precipitous canyon edges or crawled laboriously up the precarious faces of cliffs that rose directly from the depths of the river bed below. At times the tracks left the dubious protection of the mountainsides to run up graded trestles that seemed to tremble beneath the weight of the train. Sometime after dark, which came early in the mountains in winter, the engineer was forced to halt halfway up the steep grade of one of these trestles, for what seemed to be an unusual length of time.

My husband and the salesman had left the coach to try to learn the reason for such a long delay and they, in turn, were gone for such a long time themselves that I decided to go forward myself and find out what we were up against. The train had been stopped near the highest point of the trestle and when I carefully climbed down from the vestibule I seemed to be standing on the peak of one of those leap-the-dip rides one can find in any fairground. I stared out into space, but everything was black except for the bright glare of the train's headlight. By its light I saw several men at work on the rails and the night rang with the clash of tools on steel. Arthur soon reappeared and reproved me for climbing out of the train.

"You might have slipped and fallen down into the canyon, it's nine hundred feet from this point. We'll be getting under way at any moment. There was a split rail, it could have wrecked us if the work crew had not detected it in time!"

The nonchalant way he said this really made me stare at him. He had warned me before we boarded the train that it was risky and was only part of the dangers that we might have to face. Personally I felt that circumstances might have waited until the mud of Vancouver streets had had time to dry on our shoes, but fibbed a little and told him that I was not frightened. I was to learn the hard way that it would be a case of fools rushing in.

The locomotive gave a few exasperated warning snorts and we resumed our journey. The delay made us late getting to Lone Butte so that it was 4:30 a.m. when we climbed out of the warm coach and were assaulted by the high cold temperatures of the plateau country of British Columbia. The train was met by the station-master who also operated the log-cabin hotel. He was joined by two young Indians who proceeded to unload our furnishings onto the platform. It was bleak and cold, about 15 degrees below zero C. and my teeth began to chatter uncontrollably. The engineer soon sounded the melancholy whistle for departure and the train disappeared around a curve. With this last link with our former life broken, we took stock of our surroundings.

"My goodness! Let's hurry and get my cases of preserved fruit off this platform before it freezes and we lose it all!" I said, shivering and clutching Roland tightly against me. I wanted to get him indoors, too, before he froze. I hadn't reckoned on such a difference in climatic conditions just a few hundred miles from the soft air of the Pacific coast.

Gus Horn, the stationmaster, assured me that everything would be taken care of properly. "Leave it to us, ma'am, you hurry up to the hotel and my wife will get you warmed up again. She always makes hot coffee when the train comes in, no matter what time it arrives."

Mrs. Horn did her best, as promised, but I told myself I'd never be warm again. My blood felt congealed in my veins, being acclimatized as I was to the mild dampness of the south coast.

Mrs. Horn could not guarantee that a guest bedroom would be warm because all the walls of the hotel required rechinking. Wondering what that could mean, I elected to stay cosy beside the large drum heater. While she prepared breakfast for some men she called "the old baches," I told her about conditions in the city we had left the previous day. Mrs. Horn had not revisited Vancouver since she saw it as a bride when she had recently arrived from

Germany. She said that she felt that a large city was cold and impersonal. Here in this sparsely settled Cariboo country, people were friendly and ready to lend a hand to the new settlers now coming into this lonely district to live.

I told her how things were in Vancouver now, with the influx of more and more unemployed people from all the other parts of Canada. "The depression has the whole country in the worst business slump we have ever known. Many men would starve if it were not for the soup kitchens being operated by missions and hostels. My husband and I decided that better opportunities were waiting here. We're young and healthy and quite able to rough it for a while."

"You're quite right," agreed Mrs. Horn as she deftly kneaded bread dough, "here a man can shoot all the game he needs, and in many parts the soil will grow vegetables. All the land will bear good feed crops for cattle. Even though we have a very short summer I was able to grow a fine lot of root crops. I even had green peas and wonderful cabbage."

The bachelors had arrived and we joined them in the dining area for breakfast. After the meal, we left the baby in Mrs. Horn's care and went to the general store to purchase supplies.

The clear light of a sparkling cold morning revealed the first glimpse I had of Lone Butte. Courtesy called it a town, but hamlet was the correct name for this tiny whistle-stop railroad place which consisted of one hotel, a small station house beside the tracks, a large general store, a one-roomed schoolhouse and a community hall which answered all social requirements. Church services were held there whenever a minister could make the trip to this lonely backwoods town. There were about sixteen homes in all and every one of the buildings was built of logs.

Straight lodge-pole pines were stripped of bark and the ends of the logs cut out in such a way that the log set upon it fitted tightly. Then when all the logs were up and a roof added, the logs' spaces were filled with moss and plastered with clay to fill any crevices that could permit freezing draughts to blow inside. Some white-painted corrals stood next to the railway tracks, a reminder that this was cattle country and Lone Butte known as a "cow town."

About one quarter of a mile north stood a solitary square rock sparsely covered with scrawny jack pines. There were no other rock formations in sight; snow-covered land surrounded it on all sides. It was for this large, square rock that the town was named. Months later we saw luxurious summer verdure where fine Hereford cattle grazed and even saw two cute bear cubs playing on top of the butte with mother bear well hidden, but no doubt carefully watching her family.

We entered the general store and found that it already had a "hot-stove" conference in progress. Several of the bachelors we had met at breakfast at Horns' Hotel, plus a few other local residents sat around a huge iron heater which had a heavy steel rail around it, on which rugged, wet winter footgear was steaming. I was informed that this was called "thawing their feet out." The men all stopped talking and gave me, the only female present and a complete stranger to boot, a very thorough scrutiny. I did the same for them and must confess that my first acquaintance with the male inhabitants of this district was extremely disappointing.

Having seen many "Westerns" in the moving picture theatres, I had my own preconceived ideas of what cowboys should look like, all garbed in fancy buckskin jackets, wide leather chaps and possessing dashing ten-gallon hats. What I now saw was the most nondescript group of men in patched blue-jeans, badly cured moose-hide coats and a general air of personal neglect, unwashed and unkempt. Nothing there to remind a young city woman of galloping horses ridden by dashing cowboys, speeding into the wide open spaces; another dream gone west!

We had to stock up on groceries for the next three or four months, because with thirty-five miles of snow-drifted land between the ranch at Deka Lake and the store at Lone Butte, I could no longer run to the corner store for groceries, for forgotten items of food, as I had been accustomed to do in the city. I consulted my tentative list from which Arthur had economically deleted all meats excepting for one roast of beef and some bacon. He plainly expected to hunt and supply our table with all such necessities from now on.

One of the hot-stove league left the group and joined us at the counter, bent upon offering some unsolicited advice.

"What you folks need is plenty of beans!" he told us. "Don' matter if'n you can't get meat as long as you've got lots of beans. Spuds, too, gotta have spuds and they're cheap. Prunes is good, too, if you can afford 'em. Most folks up here can't afford canned goods, but mebbee some dried fruit's what you'd ought to get."

I shuddered at the prospect of his unappetizing, starchy list of foods and asked him cautiously, "What do you mean 'can't get meat'? We have heard that all one has to do for a meat supply is to shoot game, that this is the best game section in British Columbia."

"Ha-ha-ha! Somebody's been foolin' you, missus. All the dang moose and deer leave this high country in the late fall and the biggest piece of game you're likely to shoot is a jack-rabbit."

I looked at him anxiously, then let my eyes range over some sides of beef that hung in a cold storage addition to the main part of the store. But I knew we were operating on a shoestring so I stuck resolutely to flour, beans, rice, macaroni, coffee, tea and sugar. For luxury foods I had my canned cherries and peaches in the quart preserving jars. I bought some dried prunes, facetiously called C.P.R. strawberries by people whose pocketbooks would not allow them to buy the fruit that honestly bore the name. Prunes were inexpensive at that time, but I was to find them indispensible during the winter months in the Cariboo country. The storekeeper was totalling my purchases when the unkempt man spoke to us again. His manner and his information were not designed to encourage newcomers to the region.

"I hear you're goin' to pre-empt land in the 'Isch-ka-bibble'?" he positively jeered, "there's a no-man's land if ever there was one! Nobody lives up there 'ceptin' mebbee a few Indians. Guess sometimes the game warden'll poke around when you least expect him. Your wife'll go plumb crazy up in them woods all by herself. Couldn't get my wife to live up there for all the free land in Canada! No Sirree!" he punctuated his words with a successfully aimed bullseye of tobacco juice into the spittoon at the far corner of the store.

"Oh, come off it, George! The Isch-ka-bibble's not that bad," protested the storekeeper uneasily. He probably was afraid we'd take the next train back to Vancouver.

"Do you mean we won't have any neighbours where we're going?" I asked him, already afraid of his response. Before the man could answer, George was ready with a comeback. He delivered it after once more aiming at the spittoon.

"Wouldn't say *no* neighbours 'xactly. Matter of fact Ed Martin's got him a woman up there, a housekeeper *he* calls her. Then there's always the Indians snoopin' around and a few old bachelors livin' alone and prob'ly climbin' the walls for lonesomeness!".

My husband paid for the groceries and herded me away from

the vicinity of George and his spiteful tongue. The unkempt fellow sent a baleful glance after us, which I took the trouble to return in full measure. Of all my choices for neighbours in the backwoods he was the one I could do without. He was a knocker, of no use to himself or likely to his family either. George did nothing to boost the country where he was earning his living. I decided that the fewer men of his kind that we met, the better for our morale. There was to be no turning back, from now on, my husband and I were pioneers.

We could hear the cheerful sound of tinkling sleigh bells outside and went out to greet Paul Pearson who was halting his superb matched team of horses at the entrance to the store. When my husband had come to the Cariboo two months ago, he had first met this genial bachelor who had a ranch close to Lone Butte. A quick, mutual friendship had resulted from their meeting and Paul had also volunteered to drive us out to the Charlton ranch when it was time for us to make this trip. He was now here to fulfil his promise. When Arthur introduced us, Paul grasped my hand in so firm a clasp that when I got it back I surreptitiously examined it for possible fractures.

Paul Pearson was Swedish and he conformed exactly to my ideal of a true Norseman. Standing an heroic six feet, three inches, he was powerfully built, and I recalled accounts I had read of Paul Bunyan, another such giant. This Norseman's eyes had a kind twinkle and were bright with interest in life. His face was weathered by many severe northern winters, his shoulders broadened by arduous work. It all added up to the fact that here was a man on whom two young greenhorns could safely rely for help.

Now came the task of loading the sleigh for the thirty-two mile trip eastward to Deka Lake. We had too many household requirements for one load, and it was decided that Kitchen Queen and several large tools for land clearing must be stored with Gus Horn until later. We would be staying at the Charltons' ranch for three months or more and Arthur could make another trip to Lone Butte for the rest of our things. Another problem facing us was how to prevent my bottled fruits from freezing on the journey, which Paul figured could not be completed in one day. He had already arranged a stopover at a friend's house for the night.

When I went into the hotel to say good-bye to Mrs. Horn and emerged carrying our baby, Paul's blue eyes lighted with pleasure.

"Ah! that I like! Yittle babies." He poked an exploratory finger under our son's tiny chin and I held my breath, but apparently Paul could temper his strength to the occasion. "Two young peoples soon get more yittle babies. Then vee get more skules; this country not be so lonely any more!"

Colonizing the Cariboo seemed rather a tall order for one young couple, but I smiled at our new friend and didn't remind him that this child was just six weeks old, a very young settler.

The men placed our large bed mattress on top of moose-hide covers in the box of the sleigh and placed my five boxes of bottled fruits on the mattress and protected them with several layers of blankets. Then the crib mattress was laid against two trunks and I climbed onto this with the baby and was wrapped with blankets also. I would be as cosy as a bug in a rug, they assured me. I felt rather pampered at first, but after being exposed to the below zero temperature for some time, I soon became chilled.

The team was fresh and we moved along quite rapidly over a well-packed road which wound through flat meadow country for some distance, the now snow-covered stretches were quickly lost in a haze of misty blue. Occasionally the road skirted a lake, the centre still unfrozen, its dull leaden hue upturned to a clouding sky, its shores crusted with slowly forming ice that looked like counter-soiled lace. Before long the entire lake surface would be frozen solid and when covered with snow would become a smooth, safe road for sleigh travel, saving time when the roads became blocked by heavy snowdrifts.

Here and there the dazzling white landscape was relieved by dark clumps of spruce and jack pine, black etchings on Nature's snowy canvas, or colourful red willow hiding swamp or creek, enlivened the winter scene. Sometimes an impenetrable-looking jungle of spruce and dark undergrowth added an untamed wilderness aspect to the country which was so utterly different from what I was used to.

Now the sun stood immediately overhead and although my son knew nothing of astronomy, his own built-in time system advised him that it was time to eat. How thankful I was that I was able to nurse my child. No bother about formulas to be made up and some means of warming them found before Roland could have his meal. A short time later Paul Pearson stopped his team and tied feedbags under the horses' mouths and then the men joined me in the box of the sleigh where we shared a sandwich lunch which Mrs. Horn had thoughtfully provided for us.

We drove on again and after I grew stiff and chilled from sitting in one position I welcomed Arthur's suggestion that I get down from the sleigh and walk with him beside the sleigh for a while to limber up. I made sure that the baby was warm and cosy and revelled in some much needed exercise. It was good to travel rapidly along the snow-packed road and set the blood running through cramped limbs. The air was as exhilarating as wine and generated abundant energy within us. It was as different as night from day when compared to the damp, humid air of the south coast.

Later Arthur took the reins and Paul jumped down to walk beside me. As we passed the scattered log cabins and barns, with occasional stretches of russel fence standing darkly against the snow-covered fields, my companion told me the names of the ranchers who owned these lands. He told me that few of the Cariboo ranchers tilled the soil and planted crops of oats, alfalfa or other feed crops to improve the market value of their herds. Most were content to harvest the wild swamp hay and haul it back to the home corrals for winter use. Paul Pearson, however, informed us that he always planted feed crops and as a result his cattle were the best-fed ones in this entire section. He relied on wild swamp grass for summer pasture when all cattle rustled their food, but in winter he believed a more nourishing food brought the best results. My husband had had experience with crop growing on an uncle's large farm and he too intended to clear land for the purpose of growing feed crops as soon as it was possible. Although the snow lay deep on these wild hay meadows which I could see stretching away into blue distances, there were several gaunt herds of cattle and small bands of horses still trying to dig through frozen surfaces to get at winter-killed feed.

CHAPTER 3

Isch-ka-bibble Country

THE NOVEMBER DUSK was closing in quickly and Paul exhorted his team to greater speed; even so it was seven o'clock when we pulled up in front of a large log building, from the windows of which cheery yellow lamplight streamed across the snow. The rancher came out to welcome us and helped Paul lead the team to the shelter of his barn, while a kindly, dark-haired woman took the baby from my stiffened arms and led me inside the warm, cosy cabin. Arthur carefully deposited my precious supply of preserved fruit inside the cabin, and our host bade us sit down to share a wonderful dinner with them.

Here I first ate roast moosemeat and found it delicious, later I learned that it formed the staple of the diet of all Cariboo people, Indians and white settlers alike. Moose were very numerous in this part of the province and all men hunted their meat. My host told us that mule deer also were abundant. He turned out to be Sven Jorgenson and the friendly woman was not his legal wife, but his housekeeper. During these years, many women, usually middle-aged widows, came to the lonely Cariboo country in response to advertisements in the newspapers of large cities. Their employers were hard-working backwoods ranchers in great need of good housekeepers and even more in need of women's companionship.

Most of these women were treated so kindly and considerately by the lonely men for whom they had come to work, that not one of those I met in the Cariboo would have exchanged their jobs for those with city conveniences and amenities. In many cases where the couple were free to marry, they did so, but when it was not possible, they lived together contentedly as common law man and wife, and I was unable to detect anything to denote that a legal relationship would have made any difference in their lives. These women shared the rigours of pioneer life, made a comfortable home and cooked excellent meals for their men, working with them at tasks in the barn and fields, usually considered men's work. Young though I was, I had observed enough unhappy and often divorced married couples to know that responses made in church, or legal papers signed, were not in themselves the open sesame to a lasting marriage. These unions did seem truly happy and blessed.

Sven Jorgenson's housekeeper was Mrs. Mary Yorke. Her husband had deserted her several years before. She left Vancouver to come and take the position of housekeeper for our host. She said, "Truly, I can't tell you just how good Sven has been to me. If my husband had been one-tenth as kind and decent, I guess I should still be working in the city, supporting him and myself. He saw fit to leave me and the way things have worked out for me, it was certainly all for the best."

We were washing the dishes in one corner of the large combined kitchen-living room, which was the usual plan of all these log-cabin homes. The men were smoking, drawn up comfortably by the huge Quebec heater. Suddenly I heard them mention grizzly bears and I was immediately all ears; Sven's voice rang out.

"I yoost vas out cutting brush on the east side of my land and it was getting late and colder so I decide it's time to quit. So I am coming home by the trail and vat should I see coming right tovards me? A great big grizzly, almost he vas running into me! Vat could I do? I haf yoost the axe in my hand, no gun vit me ven I need it most! 'Sven, I tell myself, you are finished.' Yes I am saying good-bye world, and feel very sorry for Sven, but I put up my axe, might as vell put up a fight vit this grizzly!"

Sven had paused dramatically and Paul asked in a worried manner, "Yoost an axe, Sven? So what did you do, I see you safe and well!"

"Paul, I vas yoost lucky that bear had other plans. He goes biff with his big right paw, and avay goes my axe into the deep snow. He takes a swipe at me vit his left paw, and avay goes Sven, right off the trail and into a big snowdrift! Grizzly bear has trail all to himself and off he goes, no more trouble for me. I yoost was lucky and run all the vay home, quick like a mouse, you bet!" Sven sighed gustily.

27

"What a good thing for you that the grizzly had other plans," observed my husband. "But tell me, are there many grizzlies in this part of the country? I was told that they stick pretty close to the foothills of the Rockies."

"Yes, that's true, mostly we yoost see black or brown bears, but vunce in a vhile, like this time, along will come a grizzly yoost ven nobody expects to see him," the rancher explained.

Mary Yorke ushered me into a bedroom where bunks heaped with blankets lined the log walls. She pointed out two of them and said, "We've plenty of beds, you'll sleep well there. Now don't worry! I can see Sven's adventure has scared you, but it is like he said, grizzlies don't come very close to the ranches."

I got into the bunk where my son was already sleeping, imagining what I would ever do if I came face to face with a grizzly in the woods. Then, exhausted by the long, cold drive from Lone Butte, I was engulfed in sleep somewhat in the way one's body succumbs to the sweep of giant waves on the shore.

Later I learned much more about grizzlies, and was told that sometimes they attacked humans, seemingly without provocation, while at other times the bear might merely regard a man curiously and pass by, going about its business, secure in its belief of sovereignty in the forests and mountains that were its natural habitat. I decided, just before sleep overcame me that evening, that it probably depended upon whether or not the bear had recently dined and had a comfortable full stomach, or that perhaps animals are subject to moods like people are.

Early next morning, before Paul and Arthur loaded our fruit jars back on the sleigh, I insisted upon giving the hospitable Mary and Sven some of the fruit which is so scarce in the Isch-ka-bibble. Then we resumed our journey eastward and Paul assured us that the future promised prosperity to people who would make it their home, due to the availability of materials for home building, the richness promised by the virgin soil for crop-growing and also, not least to the country's notable abundance of game and fish.

Late in the afternoon Paul told us we were now approaching Deka Lake and the horses gradually descended a slope at the foot of which stood Charltons' ranch house and barns. The lake stretched to the north further than one could see. The lake itself was a vast snow-covered surface and on it, not far from shore, stood one lone coyote watching our approach.

This was the first coyote I had seen quite close, although I was by now familiar with their high keening voices, heard chiefly at night. This coyote decided that we were getting too close for comfort and quickly ran across the lake and faded from sight in brush that lined the opposite side of Deka Lake.

While Paul Pearson unhitched his team and led them towards the barn, my husband carried some of our bags indoors and immediately set about building fires in the cook stove and in a large Quebec heater at the other end of the large living room off which two doors opened into bedrooms. The cabin was very cold but the heat from the stoves soon changed that. Paul came back and helped Arthur carry in my cases of fruit, the mattresses and other things we had piled into the box of the sleigh. Mercifully none of the bottles of fruit had frozen, in spite of the long cold drive in below zero weather. I was pleased with Nature's co-operation and very thankful I had taken the fruit with us on the long journey. The bottles would be very handy for the future canning and preserving of fish and meat to fill our larder.

One thing for which I was very thankful was the way Roland had stood the long trip. Babies of his age usually do sleep most of the time and the bracing air had added to this ability to sleep all through a long cold journey. He had the makings of a pioneer child.

We found a note on the kitchen table stating that our hosts had been unable to await our arrival and that their milk cow was at the Hodges' ranch on Sulphurous Lake. Arthur could go over and drive her home as soon as he reached Charltons' home. The cattle and horses were foraging for themselves, but my husband said he would get them in off the range and feed them over the winter months at the home corrals as he had promised the Charltons when he had met them in September.

While the men were working, I prepared my first hearty dinner in the wilderness and we all devoured it hungrily. When I had washed up I was so sleepy I just wanted to roll into bed and sleep. The long drive in the bracing air had done this. One of the greatest boons the wilderness can grant to man is that of restful sleep. How wonderful to wake in the morning, full of the joy of living, and crammed with energy and ambition. How long had it been, I wondered, since Arthur and I had felt like this? I remembered wakeful nights when, obsessed with fear of the future, worry over ways and means, it had been impossible to sleep, and the dawn had brought no solution.

I arose full of purpose and began to prepare the standard ranch breakfast. The men, at least, must have their flapjacks, and to this I added crisp bacon and, of course, plenty of the preserved fruits. After the meal Paul declared that he must start for home. Arthur had hidden several jars of the peaches that this good friend seemed to prefer, in the box of his sleigh while Paul was harnessing his team. He had refused any remuneration for driving us to Deka Lake, so my husband promised to go to Paul's ranch later to help with the building of more russel fences on Paul's ranch. He needed help more than money, he told us as he departed. To Arthur's proffered money, the generous rancher said cheerfully as he was about to drive away:

"Hang onto any cash vat you got! In this country it's as scarce as hen's teeth, and you young folks is going to need it."

I did, indeed, soon learn that Paul was right, money was a rare commodity in the backwoods although the condition was not new to us. Here men bartered their labour for stock, or stock for seed and groceries. When crops were harvested they were taken to the town and exchanged for stock feed, equipment or any other requirements. What could be simpler or make for a life more full of meaning than this way of getting down to fundamentals? I pondered upon these things as I became busy with chores. Suddenly I heard a wild yell out-of-doors.

"Yip-yip-yippee!" the screech went ringing out across the lake, a really ear-tingling cowboy yell. Then Arthur boisterously burst inside and grabbed me about the waist, whirling me about the room in a kind of mad dervish dance. "Good heavens, what gives?" I gasped, a bit overcome by such enthusiasm.

"I'm just so glad that we're really here at last in the Cariboo, I guess!" he shouted, gaily. "Up north in the 'wild and woolly' where men are men, the women are double-breasted and the plumbing is all outdoors!"

He was right on all three counts. Men did have to be tough to survive in these rugged surroundings, and their women were right beside them all the way, doing their own work without benefit of electric power (and a great deal of the time doing a man's work also when the need arose) with enthusiasm and without complaint. The plumbing was non-existent, but the little outhouses were usually located with an eye for the view. That is, they were most often placed close to a lake shore where water lapped softly.

Pioneers were hardened to the necessity of doing without modern conveniences.

The Charltons' privy sat in a nice sort of privacy in a grove of cottonwoods which rendered it invisible in summer, and it was at least two city blocks from the house in the interests of hygiene. It had a door, which was more than I could say for some that I ran across during visits to other ranchers' domains.

We had no means of transportation until Arthur had rounded up a saddle horse or two. Although I had never ridden horseback, my husband informed me that now was the time to start if I ever wanted to leave the immediate vicinity of the ranch house. He decided to walk over to the Hodges' ranch where the cow was being cared for, and to borrow a saddle horse from these neighbours in order to hunt for the Charlton string and the cattle and bring them back to the home corrals. He didn't know that part of the country very well, but figured that there must be a portage between Deka and Sulphurous Lakes. So he started out across the snow and I watched his figure dwindle away to nothing, not without some trepidation.

Shortly after he had left a most fearful racket commenced further up the length of Deka Lake. There were high-pitched howls that ululated up and down the lake, then a series of sharp yapping sounds, to my city-trained ears it sounded quite alarming. Coyotes! I thought, and there must be a hundred of them, judging by the racket. Knowing little or nothing of wildlife I became a prey to doubts. Were they in a pack, or was this the season when coyotes ran in packs? Would they attack my husband, wending his solitary way over the snow-packed surface of Deka Lake? He had not carried his rifle, intending merely to go to the Hodges' ranch and bring back the milk cow and if possible, borrow a horse.

Thus began my first of many frightened vigils. For a long time to come I was to worry over Arthur's safety whenever he went alone into the wilderness. No matter how often he assured me that he was carrying a trusty rifle and could take care of himself, I still retained a definite fear. Now I went indoors and looked after the baby's needs and kept busy and in this way shortened the time before I could expect Arthur back.

In mid-afternoon my husband returned, riding slowly and leading a cow. He went into the barn and when he emerged he carried a pail of creamy, warm milk. "The cow's name is Betsy and Mrs.

Hodges says she is a good milker. You'll have to learn to do the milking and good milk is a thing you won't have to stint on," Arthur said. "You're going to like the Hodges, they certainly are the most friendly people, we've been invited over to supper on Saturday, so I'll go out tomorrow and try to locate the team. Charltons have a set of sleighs in the shed back of the barn. It's time to round up the cattle, too, they won't get much feed out on the range."

I could see that Arthur was beginning to fit into his new life with no difficulty. I wondered how I would stack up as the wife of a backwoods rancher. In order to take the baby conveniently on sleighs I devised a carrying crib from an old fruit box of thin wood in which we had packed valuables when we moved from the city. I lined it with discarded rabbit skins and then had a warm shelter that could be taken anywhere on sleighs.

Later, Arthur steamed a wide board and bent it upwards and fastened it to the box so that it became a small toboggan. I was able to pull this along the surface of the snow for short walks close to the ranch. It proved to be snug and warm no matter to what lows the temperature dropped, and I was able to take Roland out-of-doors in complete safety.

The next day Arthur saddled the borrowed horse and rode off to find the Charlton cattle and horses. This time I prevailed upon him to carry his rifle, if only to set my mind at rest. "There's a possibility that I might see some game, although Ralph Hodges thought that the game must have all left this high country and gone further south to find better forage." Arthur did not see any game but was fortunate in locating all the Charlton cattle quickly. As they grazed they had been slowly converging upon the home range as grazing grew daily more scarce and difficult to find. The team and saddle horses were further afield, but by the end of the week my husband had brought them all onto the Charlton home range. Swamp hay had been hauled in the summer and put up into large hayricks, protected by russel fencing. Each day now Arthur went out and forked down piles of this hay to feed the cattle and horses. He didn't think too much of it as a winter feed and planned to plant oats and rye crops when we had moved onto our future pre-emption land on Dragonfly Lake, some eight or nine miles further north.

On Saturday afternoon my husband milked Betsy much earlier than usual, so that we could drive up Deka Lake to the portage and across Sulphurous Lake to the Hodges' ranch. It was a well-kept and prosperous-looking ranch with several fine Hereford cows in the home corrals. A middle-aged man answered our knock at the door and at a glance it was apparent that he was different from the other men I had met in the Cariboo. Over the regular-type levis he wore a voluminous woman's apron, and his hands were white with flour. His skin was pale as if he did not go out-of-doors very frequently, and he had a generally studious aspect one would associate with a scholar rather than a Cariboo rancher. Arthur introduced me to him.

"You are very welcome, my wife was so pleased to hear that we shall have young people as neighbours. Let me take the baby while you remove your coat and snow-boots, Mrs. Spencer," said Ralph Hodges. He spoke clearly and grammatically and made no use of the usual careless slang which is customary among cowboys and ranchers.

The Hodges' comfortable living room boasted a most unusual feature, a large bookcase filled with books, and on closer examination I saw that they were mostly classics, with quite a number of Latin and French volumes. So I was right in assuming that our host was not in his own environment in this remote log-cabin home. The dining room was separate from the kitchen, again a departure from custom in the backwoods homes. The table was tastefully set with real silver flatware and fine china, in great contrast to the usual oilcloth covering and motley assortment of cutlery, final proof to me that the Hodges family did not live by meat alone. From the kitchen came delectable whiffs of baking loaves.

Arthur had led the team towards the Hodges' barn and presently he returned to the house accompanied by a woman of Amazon proportions. She was tall and carried her magnificent body proudly. Thick blonde braids were indeed a crowning glory above a rosy and healthy face. All this was contrasted by her nondescript garments, jeans stuffed into knee-high boots and a couple of warm but shapeless sweaters. The clothes reeked of the barn and spoke for themselves just how Mrs. Hodges had been occupied recently.

"Well I'm sure glad you could come; just let me look at that cute little fellow!" Mrs. Hodges said in clear, carrying tones. She offered her hand and as I took it I could feel the mannish strength in her handshake. Right then I felt that one could rely upon this woman for good advice accompanied by practical assistance.

"Hold dinner a minute or two while I shed these work duds, Pa," said this pioneer wife. "The kids have gone to Jeffersons to buy a riding horse, so I guess they'll be staying there for dinner." Turning to me she added, "Perhaps you'd like to lay the baby down on my bed. You can't enjoy a meal holding a child on your lap, leastways, I never could."

I followed her into a neat bedroom, and put Roland down as she suggested. He was fast asleep. That is one thing about very young babies, they sleep twenty hours out of twenty-four if they are healthy. Mine, I was thankful to say, fit comfortably into that category.

"I hope you have a good appetite," said my hostess hospitably as she donned a crisply ironed frock. "Pa is the best cook I've ever seen and I'm hungry enough to eat a horse." Apparently in the Hodges' household the male and female roles were reversed and later I was to hear the reason for this.

As soon as we were seated, Ralph Hodges appeared from the kitchen bearing a huge platter on which was a succulent standing rib roast of beef. Once again this was a departure from the backwoods norm. Most of the settlers ate only game meat which was there for the hunting. Mr. Hodges' bread also in no way resembled the sourdough concocted by most of the Cariboo bachelors.

All four of us seemed mutually interested in each other and although Ralph Hodges was somewhat introverted and shy, his wife was quite the reverse and seemed pleased to have a new woman for her nearest neighbour. She had been born in the Cariboo, raised on a ranch, and could shoot as well as any of her father's cowhands.

So she questioned me about life in the cities and found that many girls grow up in towns all across the country unable to cook because they go out to office positions as soon as they leave school and their mothers take care of the housekeeping.

"You're going to find it hard then to get accustomed to living in the backwoods and baking bread and all those things." Mrs. Hodges apparently thought I was biting off more than I could chew. But I told her my mother had taught us how to bake bread and preserve fruit and I would learn how to can meat and fish myself. But I asked her to tell me of any short-cuts to easier living in this lonely land. I told her that the thing I was missing most was fresh green vegetables. We had always had a generous supply of them at the coast from the market garden farms in the Fraser Valley.

34

"I'm so glad you told me," our kind-hearted hostess said, "I can let you have all you want of root vegetables, besides some heads of cabbage which I grew last summer. We hang them upside down in our root cellars where they won't freeze and it helps a lot with the menu in winter when fresh green things are not available, I always end up with more than one family can use, somehow."

She was as good as her word and when we were ready to go home we took with us a generous supply from their root cellar. The sparkling cold night was lovely and occasionally a hoot owl would plaintively ask of anyone who happened to be listening, "Hoo—hoo?" So we told the owl that we were new friends who had come to live near him in the Isch-ka-bibble.

CHAPTER 4

We Learn How to Fish
Through the Ice

THE FOLLOWING TUESDAY was Mail Day and Arthur rode out the mile to the mail box which was on the carrier's route to Bridge Lake. Nobody who has ever lived in remote and inaccessible places will forget what an event the collecting of the mail is. It is the one big occasion of the week and no one ever misses. He brought back letters and newspapers from home and also a letter from someone in Williams Lake. It was from Jack Charlton, brother of Roy, whose stock was in our charge for the winter. His note said that his team had become bogged and had had to be destroyed, leaving him without horses. He had written to Roy in Vancouver asking if he could borrow his team for a few months. Jack had enclosed his brother's written consent and said that he would arrive shortly at Deka Lake to get the team and sleigh.

Arthur put the letter down and said dubiously, "Well, that tears it! This means I shall have to try and buy a team right away in order to haul our equipment and the hay I've bought from Roy up to our ranch site on Dragonfly. I hadn't counted on having to lay out cash for a team just at present."

I answered cheerfully, "Don't worry about it, dear. We have a few hundred dollars in the bank yet, and we'd have had to buy a team for ourselves eventually, so it really does not matter just when."

When Jack Charlton arrived on Friday he was flustered with apologies about depriving us of the use of Roy's team. "I really feel terrible taking the team off you in this fashion, but I've had a season of rotten luck. Lost some cattle too, in a big bog near my ranch, besides the team, and I can't see my way clear to buying replacements just now."

My husband reassured him, "Don't worry about it, I've got to get a team of my own anyway, this just hurries it up a little."

I prepared lunch and as Jack talked I became aware that part of what he kept calling his bad run of luck, was mostly poor management. I began to realize that not all men who were ranching in the Cariboo were successful. It took experience and a great deal of hard work. Jack, it seemed, left a lot to chance in his haphazard style of ranging his cattle and horses and was now paying for careless management.

After lunch when Jack Charlton had harnessed the team and driven off with the sleigh, we felt a bit let-down. Arthur said, "I'll ride over to Hodges' place tomorrow morning and see if they know of anyone with a team and maybe a good saddle horse for sale. They're acquainted with everyone for miles around. Right now I think I'll ride north through the woods to see if I can spot any game."

"Yes, please do," I replied, "the small amount of fresh meat we bought in town was used up long ago. I would certainly enjoy a venison roast, or even some rabbits for pie would help with the menu a great deal. You'll get tired of beans or macaroni dishes."

When Arthur came back, however, he said there had not been a sign of game. Perhaps we would be wise to cut a hole in the ice and put down a nightline. Instead of meat we would willingly take a good lake trout or char. This task turned out to be a little harder than we had expected. First we chose a spot well out from shore and then chipped away diligently for what seemed ages to me, making a small break in the thick ice surface. Once the hole was made, Arthur used a handsaw and the work went more easily. Finally a large enough opening was made, and baiting the six hooks with bacon fat rinds, we put down the line and hoped that morning would reveal one or perhaps two fish.

This proved to be as fruitless as the hunt for game, and we tried several other locations with the same results. "There must be some way to get good results on a nightline!" my husband muttered, "I'll have to learn the secret first, though."

I was forced to cook beans without the redeeming flavour of pork fat or bacon, starchy casseroles of macaroni or soups made chiefly of turnips and carrots, never popular with my mate. When

one is without meat dishes for a long time it seems that other meals are completely without savour.

Arthur rode over to Hodges' ranch to try and learn where he might purchase a team and sleigh. When he returned he told me that we were invited to the Hodges' home for Christmas dinner and that on New Year's Eve there would be a big community wingding at Willow, given by Walt Briggs who had the largest cattle ranch in this part of the Cariboo. Everyone was invited, including newcomers like ourselves. There we might hear of a team for sale, as ranchers came with their families from as far as seventy-five miles away. Hodges' sleigh was big enough to accommodate their family and ourselves. No one remained at home when a community get-together like this was planned.

Next day we had a visitor, our second since Paul Pearson had brought us to Deka Lake. When he had dismounted and tied his horse to a hitching post near the cabin, we saw that the man was an Indian. Arthur asked him to come in and as he entered he brought with him a freezing whiff of the outdoors, as it was then thirty degrees below zero. He was tall and well-proportioned, muffled in a heavy mackinaw and wearing long-fringed buckskin pants. His head was adorned with a black, ten-gallon hat, and with a bright bandanna wound tightly about his head beneath it. He introduced himself as English Deka, chief of the Canim Lake Reserve band.

"Glad to meet you," my husband told him, extending his hand, "we have just made fresh coffee. Have some and get warmed up. This is my wife, we're looking after Roy Charlton's stock this winter."

"Pleez to meetcha, missus. Me, I'm call Eenglish Deka 'cos I speak the Eenglish. Most my tribe no speak her very good. I got trapline up Deka Lake, my line run all up side of the lake."

Arthur questioned the Indian about trapping and then he posed the, to us, all important question: did Deka know where one could find game. We said we had not been able to shoot game nor catch any fish through the ice.

"All game him gone lower down in the valleys, dis country too cold. No game comin' back to Isch-ka-bibble till ice break-up. But Deka show you de right place to fish through de ice."

After drinking a quantity of hot coffee, he was as good as his word. While I prepared lunch English Deka took Arthur across the lake to where a small island reared itself above the surface of the ice-covered lake. At a point where the land formed a small peninsula, the trapper started to cut the hole for the nightlines. He baited six hooks with entrails from a trapped rodent in his pack, and assured Arthur that there would be fish on the line in the morning. After partaking of a hearty lunch, he continued along his trapline up along Deka Lake.

Early next morning while Roland still slept, we bundled up and hurried over to the nightline. It was still dark, the sky sparkling so bright with stars they seemed very close to earth. The intense cold was silent except that every once in a while, a sound broke like rifle fire. I was mystified and asked my husband what caused these sounds.

"Those are trees in which the sap has frozen solid, causing them to crash as if they were made of glass," he answered as he knelt down to break the fresh ice that had formed over the fishing hole. He carefully raised the fish line through the opening. I was just as anxious as he was for results.

You should have seen those fish! Seven big silvery beauties, one on each hook and one which had wound its gills in the line and had drowned. A char almost fifteen pounds was the largest. We certainly were in luck! What we couldn't eat fresh I would be able to can, as I now had several empty sealers on hand and had provided myself with a supply of new bottle caps before leaving Vancouver. Next day's catch was as generous, so I sent over several fish to the Hodges.

They were very appreciative when Arthur rode over with the fish and reminded him again that we were expected there for Christmas dinner. I had been so engrossed in learning how to live in entirely different surroundings, that I hardly realized how close Christmas was, our first one away from home and our families.

Actually I had rather dreaded the day, feeling sure we should both feel blue and homesick. Early on Christmas afternoon, having attended to the Charltons' stock and milked the one cow which supplied us, Arthur took Roland up before him on his saddle, because I was still unused to horseback riding and felt the baby would be safer that way. It actually was my first horseback ride on Hodges' borrowed pony. My mount was quite docile and we all arrived safely. We were warmly welcomed and the three young Hodges children took charge of Roland and made such a fuss over him. Ralph Hodges had several new books to show me, we had the interest in common, a great love of reading.

The turkey was huge and our host had, we realized, utilized his skills in the culinary art. "Where did you get such a magnificent turkey, Mr. Hodges?" we asked him, admiring the plump, juicy fowl.

"Please call us Ralph and Anne," remarked our hostess, "it's more homey, that way. That turkey came from down on the Bonaparte River. A friend of ours can raise them there, it has a much lower altitude. We can't raise them here because when the thermometer hits 60 degrees below zero the combs of fowl freeze."

Anne asked, "Whatever made you young people leave the city where we hear there are lots of good times, to come and live in a place like this where it's mostly all hard work and doing without things?" We regarded the table laden with good food and Arthur spoke truthfully when he told them that such good times seemed to be a thing of the past. The Depression was taking care of all that. Many would starve if not for the hot soup supplied by various charities. As we talked with the Hodges we learned a lot about the country and felt more strongly than ever that we had made the right move.

Dick, Bob and Sally couldn't quite understand our small son's indifference to the joys of the festive season. I explained that at ten weeks all meals are the same, milk every time, and that next year they'd see a big change in his attitude. After the meal I donned an apron and joined Ralph in the kitchen to help with the dishwashing, but Anne came in and shooed him out. "Go talk to Arthur, Pa, we'll do the dishes. Watch the kids don't play too rough with the baby."

When we were alone she looked at me and said reproachfully, yet kindly, "Whyever didn't you young people let us know you are out of meat, hmn?"

"Oh, Mrs. ... I mean Anne, you've already been so good to us, we didn't feel right in asking for meat. Arthur may be able to shoot some game soon and we'll have plenty then," I replied.

Anne repeated what we had heard from English Deka that unless the game animals moved to lower altitudes where there was good grazing, they would starve in this section of the Cariboo if they remained over the winter.

"I guess we do seem like an awful pair of greenhorns to you, Anne, but I'm so very grateful that we have you, as neighbours to teach us the ways of the wilderness," I replied. When the dishes were finished our hostess insisted upon taking us to her icehouse. We were amazed at the amount of meat stored there, beef and pork sides hung there, along with moose and deer meat. Anne Hodges busied herself with assembling large pieces of beef and pork and putting them into sacks. Arthur attempted to stop our hostess.

"Hold on there, please, Anne! We just don't have the cash to buy meat just now. Make it a bit of game meat and we'll be very grateful."

"And who mentioned money?" demanded this generous woman, "there is no such thing as money in this neck of the woods. Supposing you were to work it out instead? I need a new barn, been wanting to get one built for ages. Pa can't do any heavy work on account of a heart condition. The boys are at school so many of the daylight hours that I surely could use some help and it would suit me much better than money." So it was settled that Arthur would come over and help build a barn for the Hodges.

When we first entered the icehouse I thought I had glimpsed a furry white animal, but it had whisked out of sight so rapidly that I thought I had imagined it. Suddenly the white streak reappeared and Anne laughed at my mystified expression. "Yes, you really did see something. That's William Ernest, a sort of pet of mine. He really shouldn't be in here stealing meat, but he does it in such a fetching way that I haven't the heart to kill him!"

I tried to catch a glimpse of the small animal again, "What an imposing name for such a tiny creature!"

"He's like an actor playing two parts. In summer and fall he is William the Weasel, brown and slinky and almost impossible to detect in the brush. In winter he wears a lovely white coat with that tiny black tip on his tail. Then he is Ernest the Ermine, very much in demand by trappers who sell the pelts so that in far-off Europe, ladies who go to court may wear ermine capes. But this rogue knows that he is quite safe here, bare-faced little thief that he is!" Anne was smiling when she told us this.

Our first Christmas in the Cariboo was far from being the lonely one that I had subconsciously been dreading. Thanks to the kindness of our neighbours it was almost like being at home. When we finally took our departure, promising not to be late arriving at Hodges' house on New Year's Eve, the saddles of both our horses were draped with sacks of meat and root vegetables.

The last week of the year went quickly. Anne had told me that due to the difficulty of travelling at night in this country, community parties usually continued all through the night. We would not leave Willow schoolhouse where the party was to be held, until after breakfast the following day.

Arthur forked down extra hay for the horses and cattle while I took care of an early milking. Then we rode over to Hodges' home where we joined the family in their large sleigh. Willow was twenty-five miles distant. The air was hushed and waiting and the grey skies threatened a heavy snowfall, but nothing dampened the gay anticipation that pervaded our spirits. Anne told us that everyone, from the youngest child to the oldest settler, attended these community affairs and New Year's Eve was the really big social event of the year.

CHAPTER 5

New Year's Eve Party

DUSK HAD FALLEN when we arrived at the Willow schoolhouse, a large log building that occupied a corner of Walter Briggs' huge ranch near the shore of Cypress Lake. In the fenced enclosure in front of the ranch house sat the sleighs of some of the arrived guests. Besides these, many more people were expected to come later for the dancing throughout the evening.

The men led the team towards the large barn where visitors' horses were stabled and fed with oats. We joined the other guests who were assembling long trestle tables and benches the full length of the schoolroom. The women were busily preparing the meal in Mrs. Briggs' large kitchen and Anne and I joined them. Here I met the wives of the other ranchers while Sally Hodges devoted herself to the care of Roland. Soon the women started carrying the savory dishes from the kitchen to the tables. More guests were arriving; all was friendly bustle and laughter as people who had not had the opportunity to meet for some time now greeted each other.

These community dances or get-togethers were the accepted and welcomed means for hearing news of the entire district, because needless to say, there were no newspapers available except those that were mailed to this lonely land from friends in the cities. At this time there were no telephones or electricity in this part of the province, so everyone was eager for the chance to talk and gossip.

Arthur and I were the newcomers and everyone was talking about Vancouver and how were things when we left there, and did the newspapers exaggerate when they spoke of the desolate times in Vancouver and in other parts of Canada. We assured them that the Depression really had caused unestimated hardships and was

44

the real reason that we felt we would live a better life here in the Cariboo where there seemed to be no shortage of food.

It would have been impossible for my husband and me to make any comparison between this feast and the sparse fare so common in large cities during the Depression years. Six huge turkeys, flanked by hams and hot roasts of beef and dishes of vegetables were heaped upon the table, causing it to resemble the "groaning board" of mediaeval times. Most of the guests were men; lonely bachelors who trapped or had cattle ranches in the district. There were ten women and eight children seated. Our small son was sleeping in Mrs. Briggs' bedroom, too young to enjoy this festive affair.

Soon we were all doing justice to the savory meal, and later, happily satisfied, the guests began to talk. As newcomers to this country we had everything to learn, and no better place to meet the people who had struggled to gain a foothold in this rugged land. The conversation, therefore, was of great interest to us.

Our host was saying, "Yes, I'm afraid those big black Siberian wolves are getting more numerous in these parts. They used to stay in Alaska, and some people call them Alaskan wolves, but it is now believed that they cross the Bering Sea in winter, and game being so plentiful in British Columbia, these wolves are coming in. They don't stop at game, of course, ranchers in the Chilcotin have lost so many cattle that a forty-dollar bounty is now being paid on every wolf killed. Has anyone here seen signs of them on this side of the Fraser, yet?"

One of the ranchers sitting near us said emphatically, "I'm sure I saw two of them snooping about quite close to my ranch. They were the biggest thing in wolves I ever expected to run across. I set traps for them, but they're very cunning and must have smelled man scent on the traps because they sure gave them a wide berth. I figure they are still somewhere in the district."

Then Mr. Briggs told us a terrifying story. He had recently been in Alexis Creek on the west ridge of the Fraser River when some men brought in the carcass of a huge black wolf. It measured eight feet from the nose to the tip of its tail. It had been caught in one of Dick Morgan's large traps and lay there motionless when Dick saw it and he figured it was dead. To make doubly certain Dick clubbed his gun and stepped close to stun the beast when it suddenly sprang up and lunged at him. Before Dick could jump back, the wolf ferociously closed its fangs on his right arm. The man managed with difficulty to free himself from the savage grip and roll clear of the wolf, but in doing so, dropped his weapon under the trapped beast. Dick's arm was badly crushed and bleeding but somehow he got back to his team and into his sleigh. The horses took him back to town.

"Usually wolves won't attack a man unless they are in a pack, but remember, this wolf had been trapped and it was just instinct for it to try to protect itself. The doctor said Dick required hospital treatment and sent him to Williams Lake Hospital. Friends went out and killed the wolf and that's how I got my information."

I glanced at my husband. Like myself he was thrilled by this story. In fact he was gobbling it up, a real eager beaver! But let's face it, I was scared stiff. Of course Arthur was an expert with a gun, whereas I had never handled one in my life. I began to wonder how long my careful nonchalance about life in the wilderness would hold up against the hard facts like these. Perhaps my father was right when he predicted that I would find it too rough a life for a city-raised girl. But the die was cast, we were here and only time and the occasion would prove if I really could take it!

The discussion now got around to moose, the largest of the game animals which lived in this northern wilderness. A really ancient man, Bill Jonas, who claimed to be eighty-seven years of age and was still ranching close to Lone Butte, was talking. "They are havin' a lot of trouble down in the Bonaparte section. Plenty of moose winterin' there, but the snow's so deep and grazin' is scarce, now the moose are breakin' into haystacks to get food and cowhands have had to shoot a number of them. Charlie Peters, the engineer on the P.G.E. train said the moose are even takin' over the right-of-way. Get down onto the tracks that've been ploughed out and won't budge, train or no train! Couple of bull moose have even charged the locomotive!"

"Oh come off it, Bill! Bull moose can be mighty ornery, especially the rogues, I'll grant you that, but I can't see 'em chargin' head-on into the engine!" retorted one of the ranchers.

"You don't have to believe me; ask Charlie yourself the next time you meet him," grinned the old-timer, "he told me that down at 70 Mile just last week they found a rogue bull on the tracks and the durn thing wouldn't give ground. Charlie put the brakes on and stopped his train and that moose just up and barged head-on into the engine. They finished him off with a gun. Charlie said it must've weighed fifteen hundred pounds, give or take a few. They had to butcher it on the tracks and when I saw Charlie in Lone Butte he told me about it and gave me some of the meat. Without a word of a lie, folks, that was the toughest piece of meat I ever broke a tooth on. That moose had been kickin' around for years just like me!"

Walt Briggs grinned with disbelief and quizzed old Bill, "I've heard that rogue bulls are big enough and bad enough to tackle anything that gets in their way, but didn't think it included a locomotive. You'd think they'd know when they were beaten."

"Well now, Walt, mebbee the moose and the railway engines are beginnin' to get acquainted. The trains ain't been here very long, the last stagecoach was taken off the Cariboo Road just five years ago. Come to that, the moose ain't been here too long either. I been in this country since 1863 and then all we saw was caribou. That's how the country round here got its name. In the gold-rush days we stampeders just about lived on caribou meat, it was all we had. But then the moose moved in and the caribou moved out, and went further north, I heard tell. It's goin' to be fun watchin' to see if the moose can take over the railway line too!" the old man laughed.

Not wanting to sound like a tenderfoot, yet being unable to avoid it, I tentatively asked Bill Jonas, "How does a bull moose get to be known as a rogue? He surely sounds like a dangerous animal."

The old fellow turned his still keen eyes upon us. "You're the new people staying at Charlton's place. You won't know much about the Cariboo yet. I'd better put you wise to a few facts of life." He then proceeded to tell us quite a number of things, to which I only half listened. I had my own opinion that experience would prove a better instructor.

Moose had come in great numbers to the Cariboo because it is a fine beaver country and moose like the same kind of terrain with its huge swamps and hay meadows, its countless clear lakes and wonderful grazing areas. Each fair-sized herd had a strong bull for a leader, and he retained power by sheer force. However, time took its inevitable toll and younger bulls contested the leader's rule. Finally a young bull would challenge the leader and in the fierce fight that followed, the leader would be defeated. The entire herd then turned on him and ran him out of the herd where he had reigned. For a while he played it alone, but he had no access to the cows in the rutting season and he grew meaner every year. Like a woman scorned, the defeated bull vented his rage on anything and everything that came within range. Thus he became a rogue moose and was known to ambush a mounted man and his horse. Unless the rider was armed and alert he could well become a victim of a rogue moose. Lacking living victims, the wretched bull butted violently against trees or big boulders. He was indeed, a tough inhabitant of the wilderness.

A young man sitting near us spoke half jokingly, "You've warned them against the males, not about the female of the species? How about the cows during July and August, for instance?"

"Tell us the worst!" I begged, feeling that forewarned is to be forearmed.

The young rancher complied, "I was fishing one sunny afternoon on Hathaway Lake, I'd caught some nice rainbow trout and was just pulling my punt out of the water onto the bank, when some movement caught my eye. A cow moose with her calf traipsing along behind, was making a beeline for me. Moose can't see too well, you know, but they have a keen sense of smell which more than compensates for the lack. Mama Moose had located me and wasn't taking any chances. Obviously she thought I'd be bad medicine for her young one and without wasting a second, she put down her head and charged.

"She didn't give me time to think, either, so I had to act. I raced up the bank and made for the nearest jack pine with some branches low enough for me to grab, with Mama Moose in full chase. I barely made it in time. You should have seen me shinning up that tree!"

"Good heavens!" I gasped, "what did you do then?"

"I couldn't do a thing but stay put in that tree, Mama Moose had the last word. She took up her position near the tree, making it clear she had all the time in the world, and sooner or later I'd have to come down. Occasionally she moved a short distance off whenever her calf bawled, and fed it. But she came right back again. This lasted for what seemed like hours. I never felt so helpless in my whole life; stupid too, like a 'possum treed by a hound.

"As soon as darkness came, I scrambled down from that tree as fast as I could and hoofed it out of there, believe me! I knew the moose would not be able to follow me in the darkness. I wasted no time getting back to my ranch house and you can bet the next time I go fishing, I'll carry my gun as well as my rod."

Danger! Adventure! All my life I had read about it. Even as a small girl I preferred books like *Treasure Island* and *Tom Sawyer* to those about *Anne of Green Gables*. I had also hoped to one day experience adventure for myself. Well, here it was, on a platter so to speak! But—Siberian wolves as large as heifers, deadly as mountain lions. Rogue bull moose in the rutting season! I couldn't even use a gun and suddenly realized what a terrible tenderfoot I was. Our host had been watching me because he summed it all up cheerfully.

"There aren't very many rogue bulls around. As long as you carry a rifle in the woods you'll be O.K."

Indeed I would carry a rifle and the first thing I must do is to have lessons in handling a gun immediately. That should be my first project for the new year, or I'd never feel safe to go out-of-doors.

So entranced had Arthur and I been with these tales of the northwoods that we had not heard the sounds of new arrivals. A tinkling of sleighbells, horses snorting in the cold clear air outside announced the arrival of more guests for the dancing. Walt Briggs put the men to work clearing away the tables, setting the benches along the walls while the women quickly cleared the food and soon the dining area had become a dance floor. Two fiddlers in a corner were strafing the air and getting "in tune."

They were well versed in the country dance tunes, having entertained at dances all over the province as the occasion demanded, whatever tune the dancers wanted these old fellows could play and were joined by a young man with a mouth organ; our orchestra was ready to provide the dance tunes, and the crowd zestfully prepared to make the welkin ring.

I noticed that several of the new arrivals were Indian youths, probably employed as cowhands on the neighbourhood ranches. They had gone all out in the matter of attire for this dance and wore the most gorgeously coloured satin shirts, bright orange, scarlet, vivid green and violent purple, dazzling as any sunset. Silk scarves of equal brilliance were worn at the neck, but this bright ensemble lost considerable elegance from the waist down, where well-washed and faded denims took over. However, the highly decorated handmade high leather boots retrieved some of the picturesque glory and no doubt had cost the cowboys a couple of months' pay. Out-of-doors these youths wore ten-gallon stetsons of black felt and presented a most swash-buckling appearance.

All the women wore simple cotton print dresses, since their few social appearances did not necessitate fancier clothing. On the ranches where these women often did a man's work, helping with barn chores as well as doing their own tasks of cooking meals, canning meat and fish, ranch women wore sturdy denims and tough footgear designed for service. I felt badly overdressed in a black velvet relic of my city life which had seen five or six winters already. Before the night's dancing ended I wished that I, too, had come in a cool cotton wash dress.

I soon learned that these people worked hard and played hard. There was so much vim, vigour and vitality in evidence during the dancing that one wondered where they ever got so much energy. A caller was telling couples to form sets for a square dance. Arthur and I had done a little square dancing, so we took our places in a set. I soon realized that what we had done was an anaemic shadow of the real thing done in the backwoods. When the caller cried, "Swing your partners!" those men *really* swung them, and I don't mean maybe. But everyone was having so much fun!

The next number was to be a polka and I knew nothing about dancing one, so decided I'd enjoy a much-needed respite. But before I could reach a secluded corner, I was being pulled out upon the floor again. My head was on a level with the middle button on a bright red satin shirt, my eyes travelled upwards to stare at a smiling Indian youth who had claimed me for a partner. "Oh I'm sorry, I can't dance a polka," I told him.

"Come on, missus, it's easy. I teach you polka, you learn him." My young brave guided me gallantly into the throng of dancers before I could protest again. I found myself dancing the polka as it surely could never have been danced before. I felt somewhat like a skittish pony, cantering around the floor, but no one appeared to notice my errors, least of all my partner. We must have looked like a peacock and a small sparrow but after a while I forgot what I looked like and gave myself over to the pleasure of the lively dance.

Apparently the Cariboo had no room for racial or colour barriers, which was as it should be. The men shared with their women the strenuous tasks of establishing pioneer ranches. The ranchers and the cowboys they hired, shared the dangers of the hunt, the hardships of the round-up and trail herding and the many setbacks that were part of pioneer settlements. When such an occasion as this presented itself, everyone joined in sharing a few hours of relaxation also. This wonderful country and the friendship of such people were now to be part of our future lives.

As the hour of midnight drew near there was a pause in the dancing, and I breathed a sigh of relief. City living had not been any preparation for the strenuous activities these backwoods people seemed capable of. I saw, as if by magic, an odd assortment of glasses, mugs and even tin cans that had once held fruit, appear in the hands of the guests. My most recent partner, a young German by the name of Carl Engels, now pushed a cup into my hand from which a pungent odour rose to my flushed face. He said, gaily, "The boss says now we all toast to the New Year, is it not?" So we raised high our containers of liquid and then, doing as I saw Rome doing, I took a mouthful from my cup. The liquor scalded its way over my tongue and blistered down my throat where it seemed to meet an immovable object. This resulted in a noisy choking and coughing. Carl looked at me seriously, "Iss goot, nein? My brother and me, potato whiskey we make!"

"Woosh!" I finally managed to gasp. "Is that powerful drink made from potatoes, Carl? From now on I'll be holding the humble spud in much greater regard!" I had never had anything stronger than the dandelion wine which my mother used to make at home. After school it was one of our chores to gather hundreds of the golden blossoms. What Mother did next with them I never knew, but she produced a good-tasting brew which she claimed was a fine tonic. And so it was in the first year of its life, but the following year whatever was left had developed a "kick." At this stage the tonic became an intoxicant too strong for little girls, we were told. Now it was only suitable for my father and his friends to drink. So I was totally unprepared for anything like Carl Engels' potato whiskey.

The potent brew had gotten past the blockage and coursed its burning way down to my stomach and from there south to the region of my legs, which it immediately converted into rubber, quite inadequate for holding me upright. I looked around desperately for something to sit on, just as my husband approached, smiling.

"We are all going to form a circle now and join hands and sing 'Auld Lang Syne,'" he said. "Come along, dear, we all join in."

I was still staggering from that powerful brew, and could count three, or perhaps it was four, husbands standing in front of me.

"Never mind 'Auld Lang Syne'!" I gasped weakly, "page me a chair, quickly! If you don't I'll fall down and go boom."

"Fall down after one teeny little drink?" scoffed my spouse, and he grabbed my hand. Carl took the other hand and suddenly I was standing in the animated circle, on my own two feet, ably supported by two strong men, singing with the group to welcome in the year 1927.

As the hours passed the party grew even more hilarious. Potatoes must contain lots of vitamins if that's what gave everyone that extra bonus of pep. Now *nothing* could stop the dancers. Presently I heard Walt Briggs asking my husband what were the latest dances now popular in the cities. My mate explained that we had never been part and parcel of those for whom the "roaring twenties" were named. We'd been too busy just scraping a bare living together, but that the marathon dance craze was sweeping the country then. That remark really started something.

"Go ahead, show us how it is done! Whatever city folks can do, we can do better!" shouted one elated person. They certainly could, as it turned out. Engels' Elixir of Joy added considerably to the gusto with which these hardy pioneers performed a marathon! Some forty couples were milling about on the floor. The fiddlers did their duty nobly, and if one needed a break, he was spelled off by the other player, but the dance went on and on.

The tunes changed from waltz to foxtrot to one-step with a maddening continuity after a time, and an hour passed, or two or perhaps three. I lost count. Gradually I noticed that the crowd had grown smaller, the older and wiser ones having dropped out. I wished I could have joined them, but my husband, one of the youngest men present, must have felt that he owed it to city people or to himself to prove that he had stamina. Alas! that meant his wife had to, also. So we were pioneers after all! It was on, on, on with the dance. The incessant shrilling of the fiddles, the heat and exhaustion began to get me down. The music was no longer music, but resembled the wailing of cats serenading dark city lanes. I could have sworn later that I was being tortured by the baleful shrieking of all the banshees in Ireland.

I now moved like an automaton that needed winding. We were the only couple left on the floor and I'm sure that my half of this terpsichorean twosome must have resembled chiefly a floppy rag doll because I felt just as spineless. But success had come to my partner at least, the crowd was clapping and cheering so we must have won, although I had long since lost sight of the object of all this effort. At long last we stopped gyrating! We had danced all night and I sincerely hoped we had danced the marathon into the ground.

It was a most wonderful New Year's Eve party, but one that would take me a year to recuperate from. The other ladies had gone back to kitchen duties for it was now morning and all the guests had been invited for breakfast. Bustle and good cheer was the keynote of the new year at Willow, and expressions of good will went with each of the departing guests.

CHAPTER 6

We Buy Our First Team

ANNE HODGES AND I thanked Mrs. Briggs for her hospitality and joined her family in the sleigh for the return journey. I noticed that Arthur was chatting with old Bill Jonas before he climbed up to the seat beside Ralph. Cosy under blankets, everyone slept except for me and my wide-awake son. Every time I tried to doze, my mind was filled with a maddening medley of tunes whirling constantly, induced no doubt by that unending marathon dance music.

After we had said good-bye to the Hodges family and had ridden off on our mounts across Sulphurous towards Deka Lake, I mentioned this to my husband. He confessed that he was being bothered by the same thing. It took three days for those eerie sounds to finally fade out of our consciousness, then the serene quiet of the wilderness claimed us again, and we gave thanks once more for the peace of this remote haven in which we found ourselves. The Depression and troubles of the world seemed happily far away.

Arthur had learned from Bill Jonas that he had at last decided to retire from active ranching and would sell his team. So my husband had arranged for us to drive to town early next week with Ralph Hodges (who had to go to Lone Butte for supplies) and he would take us to Bill's ranch which was close to the small town. Our groceries needed replenishing at the same time.

The Jonas ranch was smart and well-kept, especially when one remembered that the old-timer was eighty-eight years of age. I wondered how long he had lived in the Cariboo and thought he must surely know a great deal of the rugged country. When we knocked on the door, old Jonas greeted us with a shout, "Come in, friends, and welcome!"

54

It happened that the last word was a trifle premature, however, because our entry triggered a terrific commotion. A large home-made parrot stand had been placed so close to the door that when it was opened, this stand was toppled and the brightly-hued parrot occupying it was dumped precipitately into a large pan of bread dough which the old fellow was mixing. The parrot flopped help-lessly for an awful moment, then old Bill deftly lifted his pet out, its plumage covered with sticky dough, and placed it back upon the stand which Arthur had set upright again. The poor creature looked so woe-begone that its owner burst into laughter and soon we all were laughing, except the hapless parrot, of course. The bird soon let us know that it was *no* laughing matter, for it began to screech out the most terrible string of oaths I'd ever heard. They would be impossible to repeat, but I will say that the parrot had developed swearing to the Nth degree.

Convulsed with laughter, Arthur managed to ask, I believe in an effort to stem the flow of words to which he felt I should never have been introduced, "That's some parrot, Bill, how old is he? I've never heard such a command of nautical expressions in my life, nor such a fruity jargon!"

"Jargon he calls it! Them's plain cuss words, son. Don't bother bein' polite! My pet's a she and never laid claims to bein' a lady. Polly must be older than I am, I lay claim to bein' eighty-eight years old. But that nautical jargon she must have learned from the poor young fellow who owned her before I got her wished on me!"

The parrot, still cursing volubly, was combing her dough-laden plumage with her strong beak. Each beakful of the mess she pulled out of her feathers was cast from her disgustedly and Polly cared not in the least where the sticky dough fell. She was a bird with a great deal of character and I sensed a story here. I asked Bill Jonas to tell us the story of how he had acquired her.

"It's a long story, ma'am, and I'd best be makin' us some coffee while I tell it to you," Bill said, but I could tell that he was pleased with our interest. His was a lonely life and he valued visitors greatly. He dipped water from a pail and put coffee into a large pot and set it brewing on his big stove. He gazed quizzically at his bread dough, "Guess Polly takin' a bath in it ain't hurt it none. A few feathers never killed a man yet, I've et much worse in my time." He proceeded to add flour and knead the dough. As he worked he told us how Polly became his pet.

"It was back in 1864, and me and my pals, John Porter and Al Cranwell was on about the worst part of that whole dad-blamed deer-trail they called the Cariboo Road. We was eight miles north of Trail which was a stoppin' place for mule-trains and such, goin' to the goldfields. Lucky men with a bit of ready cash could afford to have their equipment hauled in the wagons, but everything we had was bein' toted on our backs, grub, tools, bedrolls, the whole shootin' match. Good thing we was young, I was twenty-two myself and bustin' with ambition to strike it rich, like fifty thousand other fools! Gold was everybody's dream in them days, and it didn't matter how you got it!

"One Yankee fellow thought he had really hit on the perfect scheme. He imported a bunch of camels from down south in the States somewhere to haul freight up the Cariboo Road. Frank Laumeister figured these camels would make him rich. He had studied the habits of camels and said they could go for days without water if they had to, and could pack a thousand pounds compared to about four hundred that a mule could tote. But it all turned out to be one of them pipe dreams! The camels' feet couldn't stand up to the rough roads, their pads got torn and bled a lot. The worst of it was that all the other beasts of burden, mules, horses and oxen went loco when they smelled the camels comin'. I couldn't tell you how many teams of horses and mules got so scared that they bolted and carried their drivers and loads off the narrow road, down over the edge of the Fraser Canyon!"

"Those must have been exciting and daredevil times, Bill?" I commented, as the old man filled our cups with fragrant coffee.

"Yes, there was thrills galore!" our host agreed, "but I better get around to tellin' you how I met up with this here parrot. We was all three trudgin' along, cussin' out the road, the mosquitoes and them damn black flies. This country is lousy with pests in the summer anyhow! We durn near fell over the body of a young feller layin' right smack in the trail. Anybody could see with half an eye that he was finished. Most of the men goin' to the goldfields wouldn't even have stopped. It was every man for himself in them times. But seein' as we was young and kinda soft-hearted, we just couldn't pass by and leave him dyin' there without tryin' to help. Not yet hard-boiled enough, I reckon.

"The sun had gone down behind the hills, so we built a fire and made camp for the night. We lifted that poor young man over

56

beside the fire. Not that he needed heat, he was eaten up with fever as it was. We tried to get some soup into him, we figured he was starvin' as well as sick, but he was too far gone and couldn't eat. I heard him tryin' to say somethin'; 'My parrot! Don't leave my pet to die!' and he stared at a big bundle by the side of the trail. It was a rough sort of birdcage covered with the poor feller's coat, and sittin' in this contraption was this parrot, all bright green and red feathers. First one I'd ever seen close-up. I set the cage down beside the young man, and this bird started cussin' worse than anything I'd ever heard, and I'd heard plenty! I dunno where she ever learned all them fancy cuss words, but she sure could spiel 'em off."

Bill Jonas continued his story. "It seemed that this poor man was a sailor who had caught 'Gold fever' and had jumped ship in Fort Victoria and joined the trek to the goldfields. Like all the rest of us he hoped to 'strike it rich' in Barkerville. That's where all the big strikes was bein' made at the time. But he never made it, he died that night. In the mornin' we buried him right alongside the trail. But we didn't know what to do about that durn parrot of his. Couldn't be bothered with packin' a bird in a cage to where we was headed!"

"I can see what you mean, Bill," said my husband, "you all had big enough loads and troubles of your own, without Polly."

"Yep, you're right! John and Al was all for wringin' its neck then and there. But somehow, listenin' to that little beggar cussin' them out, I come over all soft and couldn't let 'em do it! I told my pals, 'Hands off! As of now, I'm adoptin' this parrot!' and adopted she was."

"I think it was a very kind thing to do," Ralph Hodges assured our host, "and I'm sure Polly has given you hours of companionship and pleasure since, through good times and bad ones."

"She's done that all right! We sure've been through some tough times together," agreed the old-timer.

Polly turned a baleful yellow eye upon us, and shrieked, "Barkerville or bust!" then dozed off again on her perch. That phrase seemed to have had an extra meaning for the bird. The old man picked up his story again. "I guess Barkerville nearly saw the finish of my pet. She had a few narrow escapes before we reached the town, too. One mornin' I woke up to find my partners fightin' over the proper way to cook a parrot. We hadn't seen hair nor hide of any game for a long time, and were hungry for meat. John

57

and Al had decided to kill my pet and have her for dinner. I never yelled so loud. 'Leave my Polly alone, whoever heard of fricasseed parrot, anyway? She'd be tougher than a hunk of rawhide to chew on!' They was inclined to argue, so I grabbed my rifle to back up my statement. Just at that moment a black bear wandered right close to our camp and I shot him, instead. That was the best feed of bearsteak we'd ever eaten. Took the balance along, as we was pretty close to Barkerville and threw a party that nobody ever forgot."

The old-timer paused and let his mind stray backward over his eventful past. "But Polly's closest shave came the day the town burned down! Seems like it happened a year ago, but actually it was in 1868. It got started, they say, in one of the saloons or eatin' places. Some woolly-headed chap tried to kiss one of the waitresses, she backed away and bumped into a hot stove, as near as we could gather. Things got pretty confused and the stove got upset and set the building afire. There was the devil of a wind blowin' that day, and in less time than I can tell it, the shops and saloons on both sides of the main drag was burnin' up! The people had to run for their lives and most of 'em took shelter in an old adit that run up the creek bed. I suddenly remembered I had left Polly in our shack and chased back to get her just before the fire burned up our shack too! Mebbee that's why this bird remembers Barkerville so well."

After some more conversation and reminiscing, old Bill took us out to the barn to show Arthur his team with which he reluctantly had agreed to part. They were a fine pair, their sire had been a prize Percheron and the dam a sturdy range mare. Old Bill laid a fond hand on the mane of the horse he called Daisy. "I just dunno! Folks, it's goin' to really hurt me to part with my team, but I know my weary old bones have been tellin' me to hang up my boots and saddle and leave the ranchin' to younger men. Nonetheless, a feller gets pretty attached to his horses."

My husband inspected the team closely. He was no novice when it came to horseflesh, having earlier driven a twelve-horse team to plough fields for an uncle who had a large wheat farm on the prairies. Arthur was sixteen at that time and had done a lot of riding there, too. He said to Bill, "This is a dandy team and if you care to sell them to me you can bet they will get the best of treatment. I've a soft heart when it comes to horses, myself."

Arthur used all the charm and persuasiveness which he inherited from his Irish ancestors. The old fellow then said, "I

58

believe you, son! You're a good judge of horseflesh, too, Molly and Daisy will never let you down, and they'll earn their keep. The team's yours, then!"

My husband hesitated for a moment, "I'm afraid I may not have enough cash on hand to buy them at once, but I'm expecting a rental cheque from Vancouver soon."

But, to our surprise, old Bill's price for the team was remarkably low. Bill, however, insisted that it meant more than money to him to find a good owner for his horses and we got the team, harness and sleigh for one hundred dollars, a great deal less than we had expected to pay even in depression times. So the deal was closed and shortly afterwards we drove away in our own sleigh, drawn by a honey of a fine team.

We followed Ralph into town and bought necessary food and the men decided that this would be a golden opportunity to bring out the rest of our household effects. Kitchen Queen was carefully loaded onto our sleigh with much of the building equipment, and the balance was put on Ralph Hodges' sleigh. It was dinnertime when we got back to Hodges' ranch again. Anne had fed Roland a substitute lunch of cow's milk and he was voicing his dislike of such treatment in the usual manner of babies. It was plain that he considered his mother's presence a must at this stage of his life. I thanked Anne for her trouble and accepted her invitation to remain for dinner.

"Oh, what a handsome team!" Anne exclaimed when she saw them. Then she caught sight of our huge stove perched imperially in the sleigh box. "Oh, my goodness, Pa! I do hope you didn't attempt to lift that range?"

Arthur reassured her, "No, Anne, Gus Horn and I did that, I know that Ralph isn't supposed to lift heavy objects." While we were waiting for the men to come to the table, Anne told me how her husband had almost died from a heart attack a short time ago and the doctor from Williams Lake had forbidden him to do anything that could cause strain and perhaps lead to a fatal seizure. The distance from Williams Lake was hazard enough, they were seventy-five miles from any medical assistance, so they took every precaution.

"I guess it has seemed strange to you to find me wearing the pants, so to speak, on our ranch," said Anne, "but I've always done this sort of work. My father homesteaded years ago on Horse Lake,

and we had just one brother, so my sisters and I had to help with men's work on the ranch. So I'm only doing here what I've always done and since I'm strong and healthy, there's no problem."

This explanation satisfied my curiosity about the apportioning of chores at the Hodges' farm, but not about the selection of books in their living room and I asked Anne about this. "Your husband has not always lived in the ranch country though, has he?"

"Indeed no! Pa used to be a high school teacher in eastern Canada, in Montreal. Teaching was his profession for many years but he suffered a nervous breakdown and his doctor advised him to quit the city and work outdoors. Poor Pa, he wasn't equipped for this at all, but he came out west and wandered up here to the Cariboo, looking for a job as a ranch hand. Can you figure that? He hadn't even ridden a horse at that time!"

"That would have been about the roughest work he could have found," I replied. "It's hard enough for tough and healthy men."

"Yes, living in this country demands know-how," Anne said, "and Pa had no experience whatever of existing in the woods. First thing he did was to get lost in the hills when the first real snowstorms hit the country. If he hadn't been located by some of my father's hired men, out hunting strays, Pa probably would have died of cold and exhaustion right where the men found him. They put him on a saddle and brought him to our ranch house and turned him over to Mother to nurse. Naturally we all helped, and Pa was so grateful, especially towards me, that he figured he could do with a full-time nurse, which is how Pa and I got married.

"Nobody at home thought it would work out, because Pa never was cut out for the life of a rancher. We've proved them wrong, though. Our life here is wonderful and we have the three smartest kids in the district. Pa has been able to help them so much with their education and we're sure one happy family!"

Anne had managed to prepare a delicious meal, in addition to attending to her many duties on the ranch and looking after our baby. We chatted and told her about old Bill Jonas and his voluble pet, and any other scraps of gossip picked up in the general store. All too soon it was time to harness the team and start for Charlton's ranch.

Arthur picked up the reins, I climbed into the seat beside him and Anne carefully handed up our baby, wrapped in warm coverings against the thirty degrees below zero temperature. I honestly believe we both felt as proud of our new team and sleigh as the purchaser of the latest model Cadillac. We bade our kind hosts good-bye, again thanking them for their graciousness, though words could never fully express our feelings on this subject.

There was no moon, but the landscape seemed almost as bright as daytime. Countless stars shed an almost unearthly light upon the snow-covered land and lake surfaces. As we rode along, it seemed we were the only living creatures on earth, and I thought of the psalm which said, "The heavens declare the glory of God, the firmament sheweth His handiwork."

Our silent communion with nature was suddenly disturbed by a series of coyote yelps. Their yip-yip-yipping echoed and re-echoed up and down the long reaches of the lakes and my husband said sympathetically, "Poor brutes must be starving. We're not the only ones who have found no game. The coyotes and wolves will soon be running in packs."

The perfection of the starry night was destroyed for me. I had been reminded of the law of the wilderness which decreed as always the survival of the fittest. I was saddened by the thought that many of nature's creatures were dying of hunger in the midst of this winter grandeur that was so feeding my soul.

Soon more familiar sounds reached us. Betsy, our cow, was impatient of the long delay in her milking schedule, as well she might be, we were hours late in getting to this duty. The small herd of cattle and the Charltons' horses also welcomed us home. A rancher can never leave his charges for long without having twinges of conscience, in winter at least, when there is no forage.

CHAPTER 7

Blizzard Brings a Visitor

IN THE THIRD WEEK of January, Arthur decided to make his first trip to our future homestead on Dragonfly Lake, taking axes and saws in order to cut down some trees with which to build a rough shelter to house our equipment.

I went down to the lake shore to bid him good-bye and was startled by the unimaginably loud noises coming apparently from the depths of the lake. My husband answered my startled questioning look.

"That's right, you've never lived in a place where the temperature drops away below zero, have you?" Arthur commented. "The sounds you now hear are by courtesy of Jack Frost. The formation of new ice on the surface of the lake causes heavy pressure on the older ice beneath, and makes those crushing and grinding noises. Quite impressive sound effects when Nature puts on a winter show, don't you think?"

"It sounds as if Paul Bunyan had gathered some of his cronies together and they were having a game of tenpins at the bottom of the lake!" I replied. Heavy booming sounds, much like thunder, reverberated the entire length of the lake. It was very cold and the bright sunlight made the myriads of ice particles glisten like tiny prisms on every shrub and frozen drift, and even the air was full of gleaming frost flakes, a winter creation entirely novel for me.

I watched Arthur drive off to the north and become a tiny object in the distance. Then I went over to inspect our nightline at the fishing hole near the southern end of Deka Lake. I broke the formation of new ice and carefully pulled up the line. Five large lake trout dangled from the hooks. I baited the line, put it down again and returned to the cabin with the catch. I decided to bake one for dinner and put the rest in the "freezer" which happened to be just a large shed outside the cabin. The meat given us by Anne Hodges was also safely frozen in this shed. My husband planned to go soon to help build the barn for our neighbours and I was sure they'd appreciate some fresh trout.

Towards late afternoon I began looking out, to the north, hoping to see my husband returning with the team over the lake ice. At last I saw them, just a dark blob at first against the snowy background, but gradually becoming life-size as they came closer. Our newly acquired team really looked quite handsome.

After Arthur had stabled the horses and done the necessary chores in the barn, he came into the cabin beaming happily. "Everything seems to be working out just right for us," he said, "I was searching for suitable trees to cut on our pre-emption, when an old trapper came by. He turned out to be quite a character by the name of Randy Jackson. We've struck up a friendship and he's pleased as punch that he's going to have close neighbours: His place is adjacent to ours to the west, and Randy has given us permission to use a small empty cabin at Dragonfly to the east of our homestead. It belongs to Jack Winters, but he has gone to his former home in Texas and Randy is looking after the place. It has a barn there too, so I can haul the hay I've bought from Roy Charlton and store it there. I had been worried that moose and deer would get it all when they return in the spring. That empty cabin of Winters' is a Godsend—a place we can live in after the Charltons come back here in March."

I was eager to see our new homestead and asked if I could wrap our son warmly and accompany Arthur on one of his hay-hauling trips to Dragonfly.

"Of course, I'm anxious for you to see it, too," Arthur assured me, "but first I had better haul the stove up and get Randy to help me set it up in Winters' cabin. The old stove Jack used has had it, I'd be afraid to light a fire in it now, it's so rusted through and unsafe."

Anne Hodges had come over and helped us to unload the regal Kitchen Queen when we hauled it to Deka Lake but we struggled with the unwieldy object ourselves to load it on the sleigh for the trip to Dragonfly. We huffed and we puffed, but don't ask me just how we managed to get that steel monster on the sleigh again, because neither of us were the stature to lick our weight in wildcats. However, we did it. I was reminded of a phrase from the fairytales that always intrigued me as a child; the hero always did things "by dint of great despatch," whatever that meant. This must have been the miracle method we used.

Unloading Kitchen Queen at the other end would present no problem, Arthur said, because Randy had generously offered whatever help might be needed. Thus the stove left for the last leg of her journey and my husband enlisted the aid of his new neighbour to unload it and set it up in the cabin which we would occupy while building a larger home for ourselves. The stove occupied most of the space in the tiny one-roomed cabin and looked very imposing, but what was more important, provided a very comfortable heat.

My husband told me he wanted to spend a week at Hodges', helping to build the new barn and then resume hauling hay and equipment to Dragonfly. When he asked if I could manage the chores and milking at Charltons' ranch while he was absent, I assured him that I could. I knew that these were part of the work I must learn to do as wife of a pioneer rancher in the Cariboo and the sooner I could handle such duties, the better chances for success.

Arthur came from the barn carrying a pail of warm milk. "I've been looking at our fuel supply and it's pretty low. I had hoped that the firewood might last until this cold spell broke, but I think we'd better go cut some trees today," he said. "This job requires two people, one at each end of the crosscut saw, do you feel that you could help me, dear? You'd need to dress very warmly, it's forty-four degrees below, out-of-doors."

"Yes, of course I can. We'll have to bundle the baby up too, and put his box on the sleigh, I can't leave him alone in the cabin," I answered. Thus, we went out into the crackling cold; oddly it didn't feel that cold. My husband informed me that it was like the dry cold of the prairies that Americans and Canadians are so well acquainted with, "the kind you don't feel."

Arthur had already discovered a number of ringed trees, destined by Roy Charlton to be cut for fuel. Ringing is done a year or two previous to cutting. This causes the tree, usually jack pine, to die, and therefore it's perfect for fuel, when cut. Arthur carefully blanketed the horses and we began to work.

There is quite a knack to using a crosscut saw. If the person on either end leans too heavily on his handle, or attempts to push the saw through the tree trunk, the work becomes difficult. Let the saw do the work, my husband kept saying to me. After a couple of attempts I got the knack of the thing and then the work went along well. We were obliged to remove some of our outer wraps. I looked occasionally into Roland's snug box and he was sleeping cozily, even his face protected from the icy cold by a loosely knitted scarf.

When the ringed trees were cut down, Arthur took his bucksaw and bucked enough stove-length pieces to make fuel that would last a few weeks. He thought this cold snap should break by that time and we could come and get more firewood with less discomfort. We put the baby's box on the seat of the sleigh and filled the sleigh with these cut lengths. Then the patient team sprinted briskly back to the ranch and an extra feed in the barn. We warmed up with hot cocoa and relaxed with the knowledge that we wouldn't run out of firewood when we most needed it.

Next morning Arthur harnessed the team and went to Hodges' ranch to commence building their new barn. I was alone except for the baby and after two days of silence (at the time my son was not even a good listener) I was convinced that a hermit's life must be a sad and unrewarding one. I talked to Betsy too, as I milked her, but she just relayed reproachful looks over her shoulder at me, for I wasn't too adept at the milking chore.

When the feed had been tossed down to the cattle I would stand beside the barn, staring across the empty reaches of the lake wishing that anything, even a coyote would appear and let me know life still existed in the country. I could often hear coyotes yapping, bewailing the fact of hunger. This was a desperately hard winter for Nature's wild creatures who made the Cariboo their home throughout the year.

The third day of Arthur's absence saw the beginning of the worst blizzard of the winter. After taking care of the chores in the barn, I suddenly realized I couldn't see the path to the cabin in the swirling gusts of snow that were choking me. I remembered stories of farmers found frozen to death on the prairies in gigantic drifts, only yards from shelter and safety. For a moment I panicked, but the thought of my young son, helpless and alone, steadied my nerves and brought a return of my own instinct of self-preservation. I felt for the firmer section of snow-packed trail and groped my way along it until I reached the safe confines of the cabin. Its welcome warmth

66

never meant so much before. I gave silent thanks to God for His guidance.

Moments later I was astonished when a rider appeared out of the blinding storm. He jumped down from his saddle and approached the cabin. I threw open the door which the violent wind tore from my grasp and saw the Indian trapper, English Deka, standing there. "Too big storm," he greeted me, "Deka think he better stay with you. Is de boss in the barn? I think mebbee I put my horse in barn?"

"Yes, do that, Deka. My husband is at the Hodges' ranch but you're quite welcome to stay. This is the worst storm I've ever seen!" The trapper stabled his horse and returned to the comfort of the cabin, first asking if there were any chores that required attention outside.

On his previous visits, Deka had never removed his bandanna when he took off his big black stetson. But now he removed this gay scarf and revealed, to my fascinated gaze, a very do-it-yourself haircut. Today we would immediately recognize it for a Beatle Cut. Extravagant bangs dropped to his eyes, permitting vision, but nothing else. Around the back it looked as if he had used a bowl and cut off big black locks that showed very little gray, although he must have been well past sixty-five years old. A barber in a city shop would have had either a field day or else heart failure at the sight of this particular head.

My guest was grateful. "It's good to have friends where I can stay in such a storm. People that usually live here not have any use for Indians. They never want me to come in their house, Missus."

Too late I remembered, as Deka made himself comfortable in Mrs. Charlton's favourite easy chair, that I had been warned about being too friendly with the natives. But my informant had been the uncouth fellow at the general store in Lone Butte and I weighed his unasked-for advice against what I had learned about the Indian already and decided that the advantage was with Deka. "Oh, I don't see how anyone living in the north country could possibly refuse shelter to a man in such a storm," I told my guest. It was indeed growing wilder and turbulent flurries of snow now entirely obliterated the landscape.

I proceeded to give the baby his bath and Deka came over to look on with interest. "She big baby, how much old?" he asked.

"It's a boy and he's almost four months old now," I said, and lifted my protesting son from his bath. He loved water and always made a fuss when it was time to end his bath and towel him.

"Lucky baby, she not sick!" said the Indian. "All the babies on the reservation at Canim Lake got 'em measles. Many papoose die this winter, I think!"

"Good heavens, Deka!" I exclaimed, "why don't the parents call in a doctor if these children are sick?"

"Doctor fellow she come, mebbee some papoose get better, but mos' die. Sisters there, too, and do the best they can to help."

When I had lived longer in the Cariboo and knew more of how the native women raised their children, I understood better why so many of the little ones succumbed to disease so easily. The women at the reservations followed old tribal customs rigidly and *never* availed themselves of the competent advice of the sisters at the Catholic Mission on Canim Lake, or continued with the medicines prescribed by the doctor. Modern methods and hygienic precautions were lost on them and I never really understood why these women were so resistant to medical aids that would have saved their children.

It was lunch time and I set before my guest a hot dish of macaroni and cheese, which apparently he had never eaten before, because I noticed an odd look of mystification spread over his broad copper-toned face. Not what the well-fed Indian was accustomed to, I imagine. But he did full justice to the meal, particularly to some beef steak from Anne Hodges' store.

"What kind meat? Not moose, not deer meat, not bear. Deka never eat this kind before. Jus' shoot game alla time," he informed me.

"That's beef steak and the casserole dish was macaroni and cheese, Deka," I told him, amused by his simplicity.

"I dunno, but very good. Missus very fine cook, your boss got him a good squaw. Not eat better in restaurant!" said he.

I accepted this as the compliment it was intended to be, but my mental reservation about being termed a squaw, I kept to myself. After lunch Deka set out to entertain me, if entertain is the correct word in this case. I had asked him, innocently enough, to tell me something about the wild life of the Cariboo, figuring that he, if anyone, was qualified to know all about the fauna here. Naturally the talk got around to grizzlies, a subject which both terrified and fascinated me.

"Lotta grizzly bear in Rockies, but they not always stay there!"

Deka informed me. "Many time they come into Cariboo and they bad animals to meet if man has no gun. Grizzly got bad temper mos' times, not good to get him mad."

"Goodness! I should think everybody would carry a gun in this wild country!" I exclaimed, remembering Sven Jorgenson.

"Deka have bad time, 'bout two years ago, even he had a gun wit' him. I see big grizzly and shoot mos' my bullets and still not kill this big bear. Him comin' fast and Deka have jus' one shell lef', so I push barrel into bear's mouth an' fire for de las' time. Grizzly is dyin' and rolls on top Deka and crush him very bad. But Deka strong fella and get out from under de carcass. But dis Indian not feel good for long time after that!"

"For pity's sake, they must weigh a ton. You're lucky to be alive!" I exclaimed. Soon it was time for the afternoon chores and milking in the barn. When I glanced out I couldn't see more than a yard or so through the squalls of snow, certainly the barn wasn't visible. My guest gallantly assured me that though it was women's work, he would do it for me this time. Being a *white* squaw apparently had its advantages, I discovered.

I set about preparing dinner while Deka fought his way to and from the barn through deep snow. We sat down to more beef steaks, vegetables and pie and more compliments from my guest. Then Deka settled down in the easy chair, apparently prepared to spend the night in the shelter of the cabin.

Shades of Emily Post, I thought, I guess he expects to spend the night here. What would you advise in a case like this, dear Emily? Young white woman, rugged Indian brave, no longer young, lonely cabin completely isolated due to a mammoth blizzard? Well, I decided sensibly, the proprieties must be sacrificed. No one could put a man out into a storm as bad as the one that was raging now. Not being a mind reader, the trapper started upon another bear episode. This one had to do with getting a winter supply of what the Indian called grease, that is fats for cooking with, he explained when I looked mystified.

"Damn moose, he alla time runnin', never get no fat on him. Deer, him not get no fat, so people gotta kill bear, get fat off and use it for cookin'. Bear him got a lot fat and good eatin' meat, too!"

"So you shoot bears just before they go into hibernation?" I asked him, and knew by the puzzled look that spread over Deka's face that I was talking over his head. "Before he holes up, I mean?"

"No, gotta watch where bear holes up, then get him out and shoot him. But gotta be quick! One time Deka and friend John Fisher from Canim Lake fin' where big bear hole up. Then Johnny pitches torch in bear's hole. Deka is ready wit' gun. But somet'ing go wrong, mebbee Johnny too slow, bear come out fast and grab dat Indian roun' de neck and claw him face! Scratch poor Johnny's eyes, so now him blind, and face got lotta scars on! But Deka, he fas' man wit' gun and shoot dat bear dead, and we get lotta bear grease from him. Poor ole Johnny. Jus' too bad for him, hey?"

I shuddered as my vivid imagination pictured the horrid details as told by my guest. "It's too big a price to pay for a bit of cooking fat, Deka. I'd sooner do without any at all!"

"Nex' fall Deka goin' to take your boss out to fin' bear in hole, get plenty fat to cook moose all winter, mebbee!"

"You're going to do *what*?" I shrieked. "Over my dead body you will! Do you think I want my husband blinded or hurt? You can cancel that plan! It's out, completely! Do you understand?"

"Deka think white squaw too bossy woman!" the Indian informed me with great disdain. "Jus' the same, her man go if he want to go. Him gotta learn to live in Cariboo!"

This was one occasion where I did *not* feel that it was necessary to do whatever Rome happened to be doing, especially if it reeked of danger and foolhardiness, as Deka's tale certainly did indicate. I would have something to say about this method of hunting bear, that was certain, bossy squaw or not!

The trapper resumed his bear stories, the next one being more humorous, at least to him. Some white ranchers who were cattle-raising near Canim Lake had gone to town for a few days, leaving their cabin locked up. This was summer time and the cattle were out on the range. Apparently a couple of bears had discovered that the cabin was unoccupied and had proceeded to break in. Their method was most unorthodox, though probably not so for members of the ursine family. Deka couldn't stop laughing as he told this tale.

"Black bear she tear hole in roof, tear off sod and shakes! Roof not strong like bear. Bears get inside and upset everythin'. Bust down china cupboards, break alla dishes in 'em. Fin' big flour store an' bust open sacks. They even carry some sacks up to roof and steal flour. Leave trail of flour to de woods, an' bimeby people come home and fin' alla damage. Bear she pretty bad actor sometimes!"

I was beginning to feel sleepy and Deka noticed it. He suggested I go to bed and he would spread his bedroll on the floor beside the stove. He said it would be unwise to let the fires out on such a night and he offered to get up to replenish the stoves during the night. This seemed a sensible suggestion and I crept into bed beside my sleeping child and miraculously slept soundly all through that wild night.

The cabin was cozily warm when I awoke and my guest was wrapped in his mackinaw, clearing a path through the drifted snow to the barn. The storm was over, the temperature already rising. When Deka had attended to the milking and barn chores once more, he ate a hearty breakfast, thanked me again and departed on his interrupted journey.

CHAPTER 8

One Woman Rodeo

AFTER DEKA'S FIGURE had been swallowed up by huge drifts on the lake, I stood listening. Silence was almost a tangible thing now because the heavy blanket of snow stifled all sounds. Not even the yapping of coyotes could be heard. On the usual clear, cold mornings we could hear sounds made long distances off. The Hodges' home was more than three miles away, yet the voices of the Hodges' children could be heard plainly as they rode their horses to school. Today, however, not a sound reached my ears. I never felt so utterly alone in my life.

Then suddenly the Canada Jays, or as they are more familiarly known in the Cariboo where they winter, the whiskey-jacks, started a loud clamouring for food. I had, as soon as I took up residence at Deka Lake, taken on the care and feeding of these saucy birds and later I added other varieties. The air became full of their squawking demands and I hurried to get their supply of stale crusts. Then I scooped the pure white snow into containers and took it into the cabin to melt for washing the baby's garments. What an enormous amount of snow it took to make a small pan of water, but how delightfully soft it was for washing purposes.

The day passed very slowly. I spent most of it caring for my small son and baking. In two days I expected my husband back. In the evening I sat reading by the soft lamplight. It had been hard for me to accustom myself to filling lamps with oil, polishing their glass shades in order to have light in the evenings, but like the many other unusual chores, I was getting used to the change in my housekeeping routine.

I believe the silence and loneliness stimulated my imagination because I found it impossible to concentrate on my book. I stared at the uncurtained windows and thought. What if a bear or other predator were outside peering in at me, a lonely, defenceless woman? Within minutes, I was a victim of the jitters. I hastily sorted out towels, coats and whatever else I could lay my hands upon and pegged them across the blank window panes. This gave me an illusion of safety at least. At nine o'clock I banked the fires, went to bed and blew out the lamp-light.

At once I became aware of a strange noise in the narrow space between the log-pole ceiling and the rafters above. Good heavens! There was something scratching away up there. Instantly I recalled Deka's tale of the bears which tore off the roof sods and gained entrance to a cabin. But this was a rather faint sound, and couldn't possibly have been made by a bear. Wolverine? I asked myself. I had heard they raided food caches, but usually quite far from any habitation. Whatever I imagined it was, I felt it had no right breaking into Charlton's house. Every so often, dust and loosened earth from the sods filtered down upon the bed. Filled with resolve, I lighted the lamp and fetched the double-barreled rifle and laid it beside me on the bed. I determined that when I could see the whites of its eyes, I would fire. Secretly I doubted if I could hit the target, even at that close range, but the presence of the rifle made me feel more secure. The scratching noise stopped finally, and exhausted by unfounded fears and with the lamp still burning, I fell asleep. I did not wake again until two o'clock which was the hour of my hungry baby's first meal of the day. He kept me to that original four-hour schedule with which he had started, come hell or high water.

Daylight brought me courage, or a reasonable facsimile thereof and I boldly went out-of-doors and examined the roof thoroughly. As I approached the back of the house, a faint mewing sound came from the ridge-pole, and this was followed by the appearance of the perpetrator of the terrifying scratching sounds I had heard in the night. I put the gun I was carrying against the cabin wall and greeted Mirabel with some exasperation. She was the Charltons' cat and she was usually confined in the barn at night. Her owner had left me a note saying that Mirabel was *not* permitted to spend the nights in the cabin. Her place was in the barn, but soft-hearted person that I was, I'm afraid I had allowed the family pet to break a few house rules. Mirabel had spent the terribly cold nights of the recent deep-freeze we had endured, cosily sleeping in the warmth of the cabin. I scolded her roundly. "Crazy cat! You almost lost all of your nine lives last night. A good thing for you that you stopped scratching when you did! Now come inside and eat your porridge." The cat had apparently found shelter from the terrific snowstorm by choosing the area near the ridge-pole where a considerable amount of heat escaped via the roof. Even domesticated animals had to learn to live in wilderness conditions and they soon became adept at this.

After breakfast and when Roland had been attended to, I ventured out to attend to chores and milking in the barn. When I reached the corral I was amazed to see that the deep snow had been beaten down by the passage of what seemed like hundreds of cows. They went in a wide swath from the southern part of the lake from which direction they had apparently come to this ranch, and wended their way to a fenced corral in which Roy Charlton had built several stacks of hay. The high fence hadn't cramped their style one little bit, they had broken down the heavy poles that formed the fence and were now crowded around each hay stack eating the hay that Arthur was supposed to guard and use for the Charlton herd.

I couldn't begin to count them, there seemed to be hundreds of hungry cattle. All I could see were cattle rumps, brown ones, black ones and brown mixed with white. I had wanted to see something, hadn't I? Well, I certainly had my wish! I wanted to hear something; the indignant protests of these animals when I rushed into the corral threatening eviction, more than satisfied me. They all faced about like soldiers drilling, rolled their eyes and lowered their horns ominously. I retreated hastily, I could see I must plan a proper attack.

There were two saddles hanging in the barn, the smaller of which I had used the few times I had had occasion to ride and in the corral were the two riding horses, the smaller one I had ridden. But I had never caught and saddled a horse in my life. I had watched my husband and other men walk up to the mount they wanted, slip a halter over its head, throw the saddle on its back and they were all set to go. Seemed simple enough.

In practice it didn't work out that way at all for me. When I approached, the two horses moved off with quiet determination, putting a wide section of deep mud and snow between us. Carrying a halter, I plodded after them. We circled the enclosure several times, getting nowhere. Then I realized that they could keep this up indefinitely and enjoy the game because four legs are better than two any way you look at it. My patience was finally exhausted, to say nothing of my legs. This precious pair of horses had sized me up for the greenhorn that I was and figured correctly that I had no way of making them obey. I finally gave up and decided that I'd have to solve the $64 question of how to get the thieving cattle out of Charlton's store of hay, in some other way.

The only guide I had for tackling the job was information gleaned from reading about cattle ranching, or from watching rodeos and cattle round-ups in the popular "western movies." These had all stressed the importance of well-trained saddle "bronc." So there was no solution there. First I trekked through deep drifts of snow all around the corral and found that the marauders had broken down the fence completely in three places. I patiently repaired these breaks, drawing on every possible bit of my strength to lift the heavy rails into place. Then leaving just one exit, I grabbed a big stick from the barn and returned to the fray.

This time the cattle didn't even bother to send me a threatening glance, they just went on eating. What did cowboys do when a bit of hazing was on the list? Oh yes, they hollered and made as much noise as they could and for them it worked! But not for me. My yip-yip-yippee and a few yahoos had no effect whatever. I wielded my staff, prodding a few rumps. They lowered their heads, pointed their ugly-looking horns at me and again I gingerly backed away. Now I was sure they regarded one small woman as a negligible risk, I was fast losing face and this made me mad. I let out a loud yell and whacked vigorously on the nearest rumps. It worked like a charm this time, the cattle all charged for the far end of the corral, unfortunately not the end with the gate left open for their convenience.

No, they cavorted right through some of the repaired sections of fence and charged around the corral and back through the open gate to the stacks of hay where they resumed their interrupted meal. I grimly set about more repairs and better ones and went to the house to make sure Roland was safe and well, because I was first of all a mother, and these ranch-hand jobs were a secondary consideration. I fortified myself with several cups of coffee and a strong rawhide lariat, which I intended to use as a whip. I couldn't linger long in the comfort of the cabin.

Back to the fray! Without counting to ten, I used that lariat to good advantage and routed the herd once more. I got them headed out through the gate and lo and behold, I discovered that the one bringing up the rear was a cow in the most pregnant condition. Heavens! I thought, what if she gets over-exercised and drops her calf right here in the snow? I had a tenderfoot's scant knowledge of range cattle and their habits. I felt that the place for calves to be born was in some sheltered barn. I would have to go easy with this maternity case, but the rest I chased as hard as I could. Out they charged through the gate at last. Was this one-woman rodeo really going to pay off? I sincerely hoped so because I knew that I could not keep up the pace much longer. I was almost weeping with fatigue and frustration. At last I knew why cowboys used such a wide range of strong language in order to get through their daily routine. If I had the time I would have indulged in a few such epithets myself.

As luck would have it, the steers which were the ring-leaders in this truly western event, caught sight of the Charlton cattle in the next corral. Anticipating, or rather hoping, perhaps, that some such solution to the dilemma might offer itself, I had left that corral gate open. Now the steers charged through the gate with the cows following and the expectant one staggering along behind. Triumphantly I raced after them and flung shut the wide gate. I had the strange cattle safely corraled at last. I leaned weakly against the gate and sighed with relief. I studied the brand on the nearest flank, it appeared to be a leaning "J." I hadn't the faintest idea to which rancher these cows belonged, but whoever owned them was going to have to come and cut them out of the Charlton herd himself. I signed off the job of wrangler right then and there, and returned, a weary woman, to the house.

My son was yelling from hunger, it was long past his feeding time, but I was unable to nurse him after all this tearing about. I warmed some cow's milk and then remembered that the morning's milking was still in a pail in the barn, quite forgotten in the stress of the cattle round-up. By this time I was convinced that running a ranch single-handed left a great deal to be desired.

Late that afternoon I was pleasantly surprised to see my husband driving the team through the deep snow on the lake. He listened as I told him of the week's excitements and went out with me to inspect the strange cattle. When he saw their brand he said,

"A leaning J, that must be Jack Jenner's brand. He lives about four miles southwest of Sulphurous Lake. Ralph Hodges told me that the Jenners often go away and leave their stock without feed in winter, for weeks at a time. I guess that's what happened this time, and the poor starving beasts started out and kept going until they located feed for themselves."

Indignantly I agreed, the animals were doing just what came naturally. I felt a measure of compunction at the way I had handled the lariat and turned my anger against the owner of the cattle. "What kind of a rancher is this Jack Jenner anyway, to go off and leave his herd to starve? If we owned a fine lot of cattle like that, we'd surely know how to look after them. We should keep them for ourselves, by rights, Arthur!"

My husband laughed, "Ha-ha-ha! You feel a slight case of cattle rustling coming on, do you? Remote from police supervision though we seem to be, they still *do* have the Law here!"

"It wouldn't *be* rustling!" I declared logically, "because these animals came here of their own accord, actually they are trespassing! What if Jenner's cattle had starved to death before he returned home?"

A few days later the owner of the cattle made his appearance. Arthur told the man how much trouble I had been put to, having to round up the herd and repair fences, not a woman's job at all. Jenner's devil-may-care attitude and rudeness incensed me still further. "Your wife will have to get used to such things if she stays very long in this country. It's all in the day's work for cattlemen."

"Is that so?" I inquired in my nastiest tone. "Well, you get down to the corral and make it your day's work to cut out your herd and get them back where they belong!" I marched indoors and banged the door hard, woke my son and got even madder.

Sometime later Arthur came in and suggested that I offer Jenner some lunch before he left. I did it with a poor grace, forgetting for once the famous standard of Cariboo hospitality. I felt that any man who'd leave his cattle to starve was beneath contempt. I was glad when he rode off behind his milling cattle. My husband philosophically commented that it took all kinds to make a world, but then, he hadn't had to deal with all those cows.

CHAPTER 9

I Visit Our Pre-emption

ONE BRIGHT COLD JANUARY MORNING, Arthur loaded the rack on the sleigh with hay and carefully placed our son's cozy little fur-lined box on top of the load, and I climbed up beside him and snuggled into the hay. The team stepped up smartly and we travelled the long white reaches of Deka Lake rapidly. This was my first trip up the lake which Arthur said was ten miles long, Charlton's ranch was at the southwestern end, the portage where we went across to Dragonfly being about seven miles north on the lake.

As we turned onto this portage my husband pointed to some moving figures farther north on Deka Lake. "Coyotes, and they seem to be running in a pack now. There's a four dollar bounty on a coyote now. I've seen them before up here. They're out of range for shooting, and anyway I never fire a gun over the heads of a team. Some fellows do, but I think it's bad practice myself. Could be the cause of a runaway accident."

The team followed a rough road which Arthur had hacked out of the woods when he first used this portage. The recent heavy snows had obliterated this road to a great extent, but Molly and Daisy seemed to be able to follow it fairly well. Then suddenly the runners of the heavy sleigh met with some large obstruction beneath the snow. The horses struggled valiantly to free the sleigh and as they did so, the load suddenly tilted and I "flew through the air with the greatest of ease" while "down came baby, cradle and all."

The load of dusty hay spilled over me and Roland in his small box. I fought free of the stifling hay and started pawing desperately through the load for my child, whose startled cries pierced the frozen silence. Arthur had been quieting the horses and he now joined me saying, "Calm down. Let me get to where you're standing; getting all worked up like this just slows down your actions."

Trembling, I stood aside and waited anxiously while Arthur reached into the smothering hay and picked up the baby and handed him to me. Hurriedly I examined him and brushed the hay from his face. Thank God, we had suffered no harm, having landed in a deep snowdrift. I told myself that this was just one of the hazards of a pioneer's life, but I was still quaking. I laid Roland back in his box and helped my husband pitch the load of spilled hay back upon the righted rack. For the remainder of the journey I held my son on my lap and soon we had driven across the three miles of Dragonfly Lake to a steep slope on top of which stood Jack Winters' cabin. It was very tiny and comprised just one small room and I knew we'd be terribly crowded until we got our own home built on the next pre-emption.

Arthur started a fire going and soon Kitchen Queen was giving forth a very comfortable heat, even though she despotically occupied the greater part of the tiny log cabin.

While my husband drove to Winters' barn and pitched off the load of hay, I prepared the first hot meal of many that I later cooked on the regal-looking stove. I was gratified to learn that she could cook and she didn't rely solely upon her looks. This was one household possession I knew I'd never regret having purchased. The excitement of upsetting the load of hay and the baby, did not prevent us from enjoying our first meal in this tiny space we were to call home for some time.

"Do you think we'll be able to manage in this cabin for a few months, dear?" Arthur asked as he glanced a little sceptically about the tiny room.

"Well, when we cram a double bed, a crib, two trunks, a barrel of flour, plus the table and chairs now in the room, it's going to be an awful squeeze to get ourselves in," I said dubiously, "we'll be experts on the art of togetherness, I'm certain."

"Our own cabin will be four times the size of this one!" said my husband, as always, brimming with enthusiasm for our new venture. "Let's go over and try to pick out a site for the house."

The first task was to find an easy grade from the lake shore. In most parts the ground rose steeply from the water's edge. Winters' cabin sat upon a high knoll which meant that all water to be used had to be carried up a steep bank, a difficult chore that we wanted to avoid if possible. In choosing our home site we looked for a spot closer to the lake. The heavy drifts of snow made our task very difficult, but finally Arthur located what he considered would be an ideal spot. The bank was slightly elevated above the lake and from it one could command a view of the entire lake, which was not more than three miles long and about two miles wide. It really promised to be a lovely site on which to build our new home.

At four in the afternoon we started on the homeward journey, I noticed a decided softening in the air. "Is it my imagination or is it really warmer than when we started out today?" I asked my husband.

"It definitely is warmer," he answered. "I'm not too well up on weather conditions in the Cariboo, but in eastern Canada they can usually count on a January thaw. Perhaps it works the same way here. If so, the thaw won't last more than two weeks if it lasts that long."

He was wonderfully accurate and I revelled in the spring-like atmosphere. It made me impatient, however, for the move up to Dragonfly where we could start picking suitable trees for the building of our new cabin. But the thaw had some bad effects also. About the fifth day of warmer temperatures, as I was pegging out some of the baby's washing, I noticed a very bad odour in the vicinity of the house and adjoining shed. Sure enough, all the pieces of frozen meat stored there since Anne Hodges had supplied us, which had remained in perfect condition in this natural freezer, now had succumbed to the warm temperature.

Arthur came by at that moment and together we confirmed the awful fact that all of the meat was bad and no longer edible. I felt terrible as I knew there was much more cold weather to come and still a long time before any game would be available for food.

"I know what I'll do," said my husband as he examined the smelly remains of our meat cache, "I'll use this as coyote bait. I saw some traps in Roy's barn. The bounty on coyotes just now would buy this meat twice over. I'll have to be very careful, though. I've been told that coyotes are very cunning and most difficult to lure into a trap."

While baiting the traps, Arthur wore gloves to try to disguise the human scent and he also wrapped his snowboots with sacking and took the traps back onto Charlton's land where many tracks of coyotes and snowshoe rabbits criss-crossed the area. English

Deka's trapline extended up the lake and immediate shore, but beyond that my husband could set his traps on our hosts' land.

He inspected the traps next day and came back to report, his face downcast, "I've heard that coyotes are even smarter than foxes, they came near the traps and then made a wide detour to miss them. I'll keep trying, however, seeing I have the meat to use as bait." But all Arthur's efforts to trap these cunning beasts were futile. They were smarter than we had counted on.

One afternoon I was inspecting our fishing hole on the lake ice when I sensed a movement in the woods of the tree-filled peninsula behind me. I looked up sharply and saw no fewer than five coyotes just forty yards from me. They were in a small pack and I had no gun with me. Even if I had, I doubt whether I could have done more than fire it to scare them off, not having had any opportunity to learn to fire a rifle so far. So I hastily made for the safety of the cabin and barn across the lake.

My husband saw my hurried approach and I gasped, "Get over there with the gun, Arthur, there are five coyotes over at the point right now!" Although he was quick as a wink, the wily beasts saw him coming and stole away like grey wraiths into the woods. We always felt that these cunning creatures knew firearms when they saw them, and also the danger they meant to predatory animals.

The following day Arthur launched a new scheme. He went onto the lake near the wooded point where we had seen the coyotes and lay down on the ice. He chose a downwind position and prepared to be very patient and still. I watched with fieldglasses from the window of the cabin. Sure enough, before long a coyote which had been lurking in the brush, allowed his curiosity to overcome his natural caution. Cautiously it approached the dark object on the lake. Arthur waited until it was one hundred and fifty yards away, then aimed and shot the coyote. He was an excellent marksman and the bullet pierced the animal's heart.

Evening was approaching and it was growing quite cold once more as my husband strung the carcass up by a rope thrown over a low branch on a nearby jack pine. He wished to remove the hide before the carcass froze. It was in prime condition and would get a good price from a buyer of pelts who made the rounds of this part of the country on fur-buying trips.

I went close to observe how a pelt was stripped off the unfortunate owner, when my husband yelled, "For pete's sake stand back.

This beast is just lousy with fleas! Look at them hopping off the carcass." Arthur was right, too. What seemed like hundreds of fleas were deserting their host and departing for the tall timbers.

Arthur worked away at this unaccustomed task methodically enough until I heard him mutter something under his breath. "Oh-oh! I guess that tears it!"

I peered at his work but could see nothing wrong. "What happened dear? Won't you be able to sell the pelt, after all?" I asked with concern.

He continued to work but grumbled disgustedly, "I've darned near cut the tail off. Spoiled the pelt I'm afraid. Damn the luck, anyway!"

"Relax, Arthur," I consoled him, "I've got a glove needle in my sewing kit, just the thing for sewing skins. Let me have it when you've finished taking the pelt. I'll sew the tail on so even its own mother wouldn't know it had happened!" I patiently fastened the bushy tail back into place and did a neat tailoring job if I do say so myself. My husband agreed that nobody would ever know the difference, which proved to be quite correct. Two days later he had to drive the team into Lone Butte for supplies. He received four-teen dollars from a fur-buyer for the skin and five dollars bounty which was the going rate at the time.

Arthur returned home grinning widely. "Your repair job on that tail passed the closest scrutiny, dear, and that coyote netted us a much-needed nineteen dollars," he said. We had just earned our first sum of money in the northwoods and it perked us up wonderfully, because cash was really scarcer than hen's teeth in the Cariboo in 1927, as well as elsewhere in depression centres of civil-ization. Apropos of money shortages, Arthur had an amusing story to tell. One of the cowhands on a ranch near Lone Butte had shot a coyote which proved to be a bitch about to give birth. There were four whelps and the cowboy demanded the bounty on five coyotes.

The game warden indignantly repudiated such a claim and offered five dollars for the adult coyote. Acquaintances had taken sides and the controversy was the main topic of conversation everywhere, some maintaining that if the coyote had not been killed and been able to raise her litter, before long five coyotes would be ranging the country. Others upheld the decision of the Department of Game and Fisheries. We were so isolated in our sec-tion of the country that we never did hear the outcome. I think the desire to know what was happening outside of their own vicinity was one of the chief reasons the men found an excuse to ride into town so frequently.

Early in February the thermometer dropped to new low depths. Arthur came in from the barn one morning with his face bright red from cold. "Brrh! I've never experienced such cold even on the prairies in a blizzard!" He set down the pail of milk and went out and brought the thermometer from its place on the outside wall of the house, inspecting it quickly. It registered sixty degrees below zero. The warmth of the room, however, rapidly pushed it up the scale to sixty above, none the worse apparently for having hit bottom.

Later we heard unofficially from people who owned a different type of thermometer, that the temperature hit a new low reading of seventy degrees below zero, establishing a new record for that section of the Cariboo which was, of course, some four thousand feet above sea level, with a sort of mountaintop winter atmosphere.

Next morning, standing outside for a moment, I foolishly breathed deeply of the tingly, crisp air and felt as if my lungs had been speared with a dagger. "Oh, I should have warned you!" Arthur apologized, too late to be helpful. I was careful never to take more than tiny, guarded sips of air whenever it was that cold afterwards.

Thank heavens this extreme cold spell lasted just three days, although it stayed at about forty degrees below zero for two weeks longer. This was the turning point of that long cold winter, in March there was a distinct warming of the atmosphere and I began to anticipate the delight of a Cariboo springtime.

CHAPTER 10

Indian Neighbours Become Friends

ONE MORNING, LATE IN FEBRUARY Arthur and I went down to the lake to draw some pails of the sparklingly clear water for drinking. We had to break the new crust of ice that formed overnight and also open up the drinking hole for the animals near the barn. The temperature read thirty-five degrees below and nature was creating her sound effects again. Groans, squeals and odd high-pitched shrieks emanated from the depths of the lake. Jack pines and other trees, frozen from roots to treetops, crashed at intervals in the woods, punctuating the silence like rifle shots.

I gazed towards the southern end of the lake where a little creek flowed all year round because of the proximity of hotsprings, and saw a white column of smoke ascending straight up into the blue of the clear, wintry sky. "Arthur, that looks like those Indian smoke signals that we used to see in movies of Indian warfare in the early days of the wild west!"

"It probably is smoke from an Indian campfire at that. English Deka told me that several members of the Canim Lake tribe come over here at this time every year to fish for suckers. Their supply of game has given out by now, I guess, and these fish help to supplement their food supply. I'll take a walk over there and see what's cooking," replied my husband.

The Indians must be desperate for food, I thought, if they come so far just to get suckers. These fish are so bony we found them almost impossible to eat, but apparently the natives were not able to be finicky in their choice of available food.

He came back to report that there were some forty Indians at the fishing camp, among them several women with young

84

children. "The sucker run is on! You should see those men spear the fish out of the creek and toss them on the bank. They work like lightning. The women clean the suckers and split them and smoke them on the spot. They plant strong stakes and suspend willow branches between the stakes and hang the fish over a slow fire that they build underneath. This preserves the fish so they can take it back to their homes later. The women asked if we could spare any milk for the children. I told them they could have all the skim milk they wanted. So it's likely some of the women will be calling on you."

Sure enough, next morning, two figures approached the cabin from the direction of the fishing camp. When they arrived at Charlton's house I saw that one of the two women was very old. She was extremely bent and required the support of a sturdy staff. Her face, the colour and texture of dark brown leather, was criss-crossed with wrinkles. But her eyes were incredibly bright and black and, I was soon to learn, missed very little of what took place around her.

I learned later that my visitor was Mrs. Johnny, the chieftain-ess of the Canim Lake tribe, the chief having died some years previously; she was the mother of our friend English Deka, and at that time Mrs. Johnny was 103. I never ceased to be amazed and impressed by her vitality.

The younger woman carried two large cans and she said shyly, "Your boss man say we can get milk here? No take cow to fishing camp, too far."

I told her that they could have all the milk they could carry and asked them inside. They entered somewhat diffidently and I remembered then that Mrs. Charlton never asked the natives into her home; I guessed that she had had differences of opinion with the Indians at some time, but I consoled myself with the old adage that "What the eye cannot see, the heart does not grieve over!" The matriarch's eyes made a quick inventory of the room and its contents, but she did not speak, and with a sigh seated herself in the comfortable rocking chair.

Soon it was lunch time and I sat them down at the table and offered them one of my old standbys, a dish of macaroni and cheese; we had been without meat since the January thaw had ruined our store. I realized my mistake as I saw the old woman try to get some macaroni into her withered mouth. "Ugh! Slippery stuff! Indian woman not eat that. Get bread, mebbee." Mrs. Johnny looked at me with eyes full of distrust. She must have thought the strange white woman had designs upon her life. Hurriedly I sliced up newly-baked bread which the old lady did approve of, judging by the way she ate several slices in rapid succession.

When I had first started bread-making upon my arrival at Deka Lake I had had some unfortunate results. I usually started the yeast the evening before I intended to bake bread, but when the extreme cold spell hit us, the yeast had apparently died at dawn and the later additions of flour did not rise into the expected plump loaves and what did come out of the oven was real hardtack. I was discouraged and my husband's jocular remarks that he could use this bread in place of bullets did not amuse me. But I ransacked my collection of recipes until I found one in which the entire bread-making process was completed in one day. From that time on my bread was good and I never had to apologize when a neighbour dropped in and shared a meal with us.

When Mrs. Johnny had eaten almost a loaf, she rubbed the shrunken part of her anatomy which passed for a stomach. "Good! Very good bread! Me buy lotta loafs every day for my people at the camp." She turned those beady, bright eyes upon me astutely and added, "I pay five cents for one loaf. Got forty people at camp, need lotta loafs."

"Oh no! I don't want to sell bread to your people," I told her hastily. "It costs more than that to make a loaf. My husband has to bring all our supplies from Lone Butte, over thirty miles. I can't possibly supply you with bread!"

The matriarch was just as positive. "Me buy lotta loafs, five cents each!" she insisted stubbornly, and added something in her tribal tongue to the young woman whose name I learned afterwards was Mrs. Lily David.

Lily haltingly explained that the women at the camp were so busy curing fish they did not have time to bake bread and wanted to buy a regular supply from me as long as they remained in the camp.

I looked at the old woman with exasperation. "No, Mrs. Johnny! I'm very sorry but I simply can't afford to bake bread for forty people and sell it for five cents a loaf. I'm not running a store."

The old crone got up and stumped over to the rocking chair. "Me stayin' here till I get lotta loafs, white woman!" she said sullenly.

We seemed to have arrived at an impasse and I began to understand better Mrs. Charlton's aversion to entertaining natives. I felt a little guilty about my growing dislike of this old woman, but before long I was able to excuse this feeling too.

It was warm indoors and the old crone huddled close to the Quebec heater which was delivering considerable heat. A very obnoxious smell began to pervade the room. It was much worse in the vicinity of my ancient guest, and I instigated a little motion of my own. At some time I had read of a strange dance performed by a remote African tribe, in which the dancers came slowly forward and then danced as slowly backwards. I now began to imitate that dance with the exception that my steps always retreated. Inch by inch I gave ground. Rude? I'll grant you that, but that pungent odour was the *most* powerful inducement. Plainly the old woman and baths had long been strangers. I simply couldn't stand the smell.

When we had first arrived at Deka Lake I had been intrigued by some quaint little cubicles that were built of small stones and dotted around the shores of the lake. They were about four feet high, entirely enclosed and had one small door. "What in the world are these used for, Arthur?" I had once asked him.

"The natives use them to take a steam bath. First they make a wood fire inside the hut and heat the stones which have been cemented together with rough clay. Then the embers are withdrawn and an Indian steps inside the hut in the nude. An obliging companion then pours water over the outside of the hot cubicle which creates plenty of steam inside. Sounds a bit rudimentary, I admit, but they are used when frozen lakes make it impossible to bathe in the usual fashion."

"Surely they don't use them when it is forty degrees below zero? Our improvised tub in front of the kitchen stove has seemed primitive enough for bathing purposes, but brrh! Imagine getting undressed out-of-doors in such temperatures!" I had answered.

Evidently my aged guest had long since thrown out the steam bath and it was a fair guess that even summer temperatures had not tempted her to bathe in the lakes either. As the old woman sat there and sat there, I longed for the visit to end. I went to the tall milk cans and filled Lily's two containers with skim milk and set it beside the door, intimating, I hoped, that they could go with my blessing at any time. Lily got the idea, but Mrs. Johnny scowled and seemed inclined to wait it out.

The delay was getting to be monotonous as I could find no kind of chit-chat with which to entertain my visitors, as I could have done had they been women of my own race. Finally Lily said something in the tribal dialect that sounded impatient to my ears, but whatever it was, it worked. The old lady slowly got to her feet and grasped her staff. She was determined to have the last word, however, for as she went out of the house she gave me a baleful glare and muttered, "White woman damn lazy, no bake bread for tribe!"

I forgave her that uncharitable dig, so pleased was I to get them out of the house. I only hoped that when Lily came again for milk she would leave the ancient woman at the camp. Before they had even reached the lake edge, I was busily throwing open all six windows of the cabin. I flung open the door also, admitting clean fresh air into the odorous interior. My husband, who had been absent during the day, stepped inside while all this was going on. "What's the bright idea?" he shouted. "You trying to heat all outdoors? Do you realize it is thirty below right now?" He stopped the lecture and sniffed mightily. "For the love of pete, what's that terrible smell?"

"Think nothing of it, dear!" I assured him airily, "you don't know what you've been missing! I've just been entertaining two ladies from the fishing camp. One was a centenarian and I'll wager she signed off baths fifty years ago! I'm afraid I got myself into her bad books, too, because I refused to supply the forty people at the camp with loaves of bread at five cents apiece."

"Well, can you beat that? Maybe Mrs. Charlton has good reasons for her attitude towards the Indians. Roy's wife would hit the ceiling if she knew you had invited them into her house. I remember she was very positive about that when I met her last fall," my husband reminded me. "We'll have to keep mum about the whole thing." I had already decided that discretion in this case was better than the whole truth.

"When we get into our own home we can please ourselves and if you'll remember, you asked me to try to get along with the natives. I believe most of them appreciate kindness, but I hope my hospitality does not have to include Mrs. Johnny too often. Let's not worry about Mrs. Charlton. I don't think they'd have come here if she had been at home," I answered thoughtfully.

Two days later I saw two figures approaching over the ice, but this time Lily arrived with a small daughter of about three years.

The child clung to her skirts while Lily carried two large cans. When they entered the cabin, I was startled to see strapped on her back one of those cradles used by native mothers to carry small babies. While the little girl stared about her with amazed eyes I realized that this was her first visit to a white person's home. Lily unfastened the thongs which bound the cradle to her shoulders and lifted out a tiny baby.

"Goodness, Lily! How are you ever going to pack two cans of milk to the camp and manage two small children?" I asked her.

"It's not'ing! All the women in tribe work hard alla time!" the young woman assured me. I knew this was true. After we talked for a short time, my small son made it known that he must have sustenance and I picked up the child from his crib to breast-feed him. Lily said her baby also required food and followed my example. There was a vast difference in size between the two babies and I asked the Indian girl how old her son was. She told me he was seven months old, three months older than my baby and weighed only about half as much. He looked too thin and undernourished, even to my inexperienced eyes. He grasped his mother's breasts hungrily with spidery thin hands and was quite unsatisfied when she finally laid him on the couch beside her and beckoned to her small daughter standing near.

I was amazed to see the three-year-old girl commence to nurse at her mother's breast as matter of factly as if it were an everyday occurrence, which it undoubtedly was. I could not restrain myself from reprimanding her. "Whatever are you letting her nurse for, Lily? She's more than three years old, isn't she? How do you expect to feed your baby properly if you allow this sort of thing to go on?"

The young Indian woman looked at me puzzled. "Alla women in my tribe do this—not get more babies too quick that way!"

"Not a very effective method of birth control is it? Your new baby happened along anyway and now you're starving him while you're trying to nurse both children! Can't you understand how foolish it is, Lily?"

She shrugged her shoulders helplessly and looked at her crying baby boy. "What else can I do, Missus? My girl—he won't eat other food. Just wants my milk alla time!" I was getting used by this time to the odd mix-up of pronouns. The Indians in this vicinity always used he for she and vice versa and at first I had found it bewildering.

"What is your daughter's name, Lily?" I asked her.

"He called Susie, but not understan' white people's words."

"Susie, please come over here to the table," I spoke firmly to the child and with big, frightened eyes she obeyed me and a little nervously accepted a sugar-coated cookie from my hand. I lifted her onto a chair and placed a plate full of cookies before her and then joined Lily on the couch. Before long the child had finished all the cookies and I said to her mother, "You see, Lily, she requires something else for food also. You have just been following a foolish custom. If you'll take my advice you'll forget it. Both children are suffering from malnutrition!" Observing her perplexed look, I translated this into words that she could understand.

"They are both starved and don't weigh enough. I'll give you some porridge oats to take back with you. You must cook this and give them both some every day. You could eat some yourself with quite a lot of benefit, Lily, you seem to be underweight, too. You are much too active to be nursing a baby. Can't you take it easy for a while, let some other woman carry the milk cans to camp?"

I had no way of ascertaining, from the stoical look on Lily's thin face, whether my lecture on child care was making any impression at all. Both mother and child did full justice to a hearty lunch of Irish stew which I served them, and as they took their departure, I again insisted, "You see, Lily, your little girl will eat anything. You must keep your milk just for the baby and you'll find they both grow a lot stronger."

I sympathized with her as I watched her trudge back across the ice, her baby strapped to her back, the little girl tugging at her skirts and two heavy cans of milk in her hands. She should not have had to work so hard. As I watched her difficult life, in action, I recalled girls of my acquaintance raised in a city who had never been required to lift a finger about the house, yet found things to complain about. They certainly didn't stack up very well compared to these Indian women. White women like myself, who undertook to live a pioneer's life alongside their husbands, expected to have to work hard at first, but when established, hoped to be able to have an easier time. Native women started out doing heavy tasks as little girls, and continued throughout their lives to work harder than the males in the tribes. I certainly didn't approve of this old Indian custom.

For a few days after that none of the Indian women came to

our cabin and I wondered rather unhappily if my penny lecture to Lily David on child care had offended the Indian woman. I had intended only to help her and tried to advise her solely on account of their health. Most of the women of the Canim Lake Reservation came into contact with the kindly nuns at the Roman Catholic Mission at Canim Lake and no doubt some followed their advice, but it appeared that Lily had never questioned the ancient customs of her tribe and had adhered slavishly to them, to the detriment of her family's well-being. Well, I had done what I could to help, even if it had been taken the wrong way. The advantages of civilization took hold slowly in these isolated areas of the country.

Five days later Lily appeared again, this time alone. She was in a great state of perturbation and as soon as she came into the cabin she anxiously inquired, "Missus, you got any Epsom Salts?" Her dark eyes were big and frightened and I hurried to inspect my supply of medicines. There were no Epsom Salts.

"No, Lily, I'm sorry I haven't any. Why do you need them?"

"Old Mrs. Johnny—he very sick. Rollin' aroun' on de ground, he got belly ache, goin' to die for sure! Old woman said I mus' ask white woman for Epsom Salts to make her pain go away."

"Good heavens, Lily! I'm not sure I should send her salts or any kind of purgatives. If this happens to be an attack of appendicitis, taking salts would just about kill her. Did she eat something that upset her, do you suppose?" I asked the girl.

"Old woman no got appendix, doctor cut him out forty years ago. Old woman eat beaver tail, not very fresh, I think."

I knew something of this custom also. When food was in short supply, the natives often ate the most suspect kind of meat, but evidently there was a limit to what a one-hundred-year-old stomach could digest. I hunted through my medicine cupboard and came up with a bottle of Kruschen Salts. I put a quantity of these into a small container and told Lily the amount to be used. She collected her milk and hurried back to the camp.

The next four days passed slowly. Arthur had not been on hand to give any advice, having gone to Paul Pearson's ranch to help build a fence in return for his friend's help in moving us out to Deka Lake with our belongings. I was beset by misgivings. What if the Indian girl had been misinformed about Mrs. Johnny's ailment? If it really were appendicitis, a purgative could well be the finish of her. After all, the chieftainess was one hundred and three years old. I had a feeling that I might be in real trouble if something I had prescribed caused her actual death.

But six days later Lily appeared again on my doorstep and my misgivings disappeared as soon as I asked after Mrs. Johnny's health. "Oh yes, Missus! Old woman very happy. He eat salts white woman sent and now he all better. Old woman's up and dancin' around de camp jus' like mountain goat!" Lily asserted.

I tried in vain to picture a female centenarian ever being as agile as a mountain goat. I'd heard of *their* prowess on rocky slopes and the breed known in the Cariboo were better than most. I almost laughed aloud as I recollected having seen an advertisement for Kruschens Salts depicting an elderly but agile man leaping over some object. He seemed to be about eighty years old! What a marvellous testimonial Mrs. Johnny could offer the manufacturers. It set *my* mind at rest too, and also established something of a reputation for me with the old lady's tribe, as I was soon to discover. They looked upon my very elementary medical knowledge as the basis for regarding Charlton's home as a veritable first-aid station in the wilderness.

Just a short time after Lily had reported her tribeswoman's remarkable recovery, a young Indian fellow arrived in a terrific rush on horseback. As he got carefully out of the saddle I saw that he was carrying a small boy. He rushed with his burden over to the cabin and gasped out his fear and concern. "My son, she sick! Mebbee she dyin'. Lily say bring boy to white woman!"

When I examined the child and noted his glassy eyes and almost unconscious state, I had a moment's faintness myself. It was awful to be saddled with having to make a decision that might mean life or death to this little boy! My knowledge of first-aid was so rudimentary and I could see at once that this case was a desperate one. "What happened to your son? Did he eat or drink something wrong?" I asked the excited young father.

"Me not know what kid eat, or mebbee drink. Me not know!" It was apparent the Indian could not help. It must be a case of food poisoning, surely? With trembling hands I opened my book, *What To Do Before The Doctor Comes.* What a fantasy that was! The nearest doctor was one hundred miles away. Hastily I located the section devoted to Poisons and Antidotes. The thing to do was to give an emetic. I didn't even know what I was supposed to be treating the boy for! I found I did not have many of the items mentioned in the book. I suddenly remembered that for some poisons, mustard mixed with warm water and administered to a patient would produce results. Mustard was one ingredient I did have. Hurriedly I mixed a solution and asked the father to hold his son so that I could get the child to swallow the liquid.

It was a desperate business, trying to get the small boy to take the emetic, but somehow I got it down his throat. In a moment he was vomiting and soon brought up the poisoned food that had made him ill. Once the danger was over, physical discomfort overwhelmed the little boy and soon he was yelling lustily. I took that as a good sign and mixed some bicarbonate of soda in water and with some coaxing I managed to get the child to swallow it. This simple remedy completed the cure. I handed the little boy to his father. "He'll be all right now, but *do* try to watch what he eats or drinks from now on, won't you?" I said to the Indian, feeling somewhat like an old weathered country doctor.

The young father, however, was absorbed in his son, clasping him closely in his arms. When he turned to me, tears of gratitude stood in his dark eyes. "I never forget what white woman do for Indian boy. I do what white woman say. He good to Indians. Some day I get chance to do somet'ing for little white mother!"

The father placed his son carefully in the saddle and leaped lithely up behind him. Then, before riding away he again said, "Indian fella very happy, not forget white woman's help." I heaved a sigh of relief and said a grateful prayer for the help I had received from the one Great Source of knowledge. Without this gift or intuition as some people phrase it, I could never have found just the right thing to do at the exact right time.

There was an inner satisfaction that comes from being able to help others. I felt a certain confidence that I could really come to grips with this tough country, where death sometimes lurked idly in unsuspected places. I suddenly felt exhilarated and absolutely sure that I had the makings of a pioneer and that I would soon feel completely at home in my wilderness surroundings.

CHAPTER 11

Visit to the Lazy J Ranch

THE THIRD WEEK OF FEBRUARY, Arthur returned from Paul Pearson's ranch where he had been helping to build russel fences. He had also helped cut large blocks of ice which were hauled to an icehouse so that meat and fish could be kept during summer months. Arthur decided that we should cut a supply for Charlton's use as the ice was now at its best. This was the only method used in the backwoods for preserving game or fish. We would build one at Dragonfly after we had moved up there to live.

For three or four days we laboured at this task, sawing the ice blocks and levering them onto a stone boat which the horses hauled to Charlton's icehouse near the main cabin. While we worked I related to my husband everything that had happened when he was away, giving him a full account of my dealings with the Indians from the fishing camp. "So they're calling you 'Little White Mother' are they?" Arthur laughed, "next thing you know they'll be wanting to induct you into the tribe!"

"What's so queer about that?" I asked, a teeny bit ruffled. "Some very important people have been inducted into certain Indian tribes. I'm thankful to be on such good terms with them. We shall have more Indian neighbours than white people when we go up into the Isch-ka-bibble to live, so it will be much better to have them for friends than the opposite," I remarked. Arthur was actually quite pleased that I was fitting in so well, and said so.

"I was just teasing you, dear. You're quite right, we can learn a lot from the natives that one can't find in books." It was time for us to think about purchasing our own cow, so we paid a visit to the Hodges to try and learn of anyone who would be selling a milk cow.

94

"Well, where have you young people been hiding for the past month? We've missed having you call," said Anne Hodges and turning to me, "Pa has just received a box of books that I know you'll want to borrow." Ralph Hodges and I belonged to what the local residents termed the "bookworm society."

"We've been very busy, I never dreamed that time could fly the way it does in this country. I had rather expected it to drag a little, in winter at least," Arthur explained. "I've been at Paul Pearson's place and my better half has been using the time to get in solid with the Indians from Canim Lake Reserve."

I told the Hodges about the events of the past month and they were amused, although they certainly agreed with me that the Indians appreciated favours done for them and I would likely be glad of the fact that I could help them. Anne thought that Jack Jenner might be able to sell us a milk cow. She gave us details on how to get to the Lazy J Ranch and offered to take care of our son and lend us riding horses to take a short-cut across country rather than drive the long way around by road. As we rode off Anne called after us, "You can't miss it. Never was a place more aptly named. It looks as if the wrath of God had fallen upon it!"

Sparkplug, the horse which the Hodges had lent me, was not a docile creature, so being greener in the saddle than anywhere else, I not only got a death-grip on the reins but also laid hold of the saddlehorn which was, in my opinion, the most redeeming feature of the western type saddle, and sat stiffly as if I were carved out of wood. My husband saw me gripping the saddlehorn as if my life depended upon it and laughed heartily. He would! He rode as if born in a saddle. "For the love of pete, relax! You'll never be able to ride unless you relax. You won't fall off! Put your trust in your mount, he knows what he's doing. Even if you were thrown off you would come to no harm, the snow is waist-deep here anyway."

I tried to follow his advice, releasing my tight grip on the saddlehorn and sitting more easily in the saddle, and soon found riding not nearly so tiring. Thank God, since this was going to be my future means of travelling, and if I couldn't do it with ease I'd be a perpetually stiff, aching woman! Before long we came upon some miles of fencing, which when first built had been strong and capable of doing what they were there for. But years of neglect and unrepaired breakages now rendered these fences useless. Then we saw two very dilapidated log buildings, one surrounded by a broken-down corral. The smaller of the two shabby buildings must be the house, we decided because Anne's description certainly fit. We had indeed arrived at the Jenners' Lazy J Ranch.

There seemed to be no sign of human habitation as we drew near, although we could hear the discontented lowing of cattle nearby, proclaiming the need of feed or water. Suddenly a movement caught my eye and I saw not only a shabby little privy but also its occupant, because in keeping with the general air of neglect, this rural convenience boasted no door. From this position of vantage the person addressed us thus, "Hello folks, go right inside. Maisie's up, I hope; if not, go in and get her out of bed!"

This, for some reason, tickled my husband's sense of humour and he started chuckling as we obeyed the man, but my face was a horrible peony red and I hastily averted my eyes in embarrassment. Imagine anyone, even miles from civilization, having a privy with no door, slap bang against the front door of one's house! The four broken steps leading to the door canted higher on one side and the door itself hung by one hinge. I agreed with Anne Hodges in saying this ranch was well named. Lazy J was the name for it! J was for Jenner, I suppose, the rest of the title quite evidently suitable.

A slatternly young woman answered our knock, her appearance as frowsy as the large room into which she ushered us. Apparently her brush and comb were having a feud with her tousled hair and her potentially pretty face bore the smudgy vestiges of make-up. Maisie Jenner was the only woman I met in the backwoods who used cosmetics at all. A soiled housecoat did not completely hide a rumpled nightgown, but none of this embarrassed the young woman. "Land sakes! You're the first visitors we've had in a month of Sundays!" she exclaimed. "You must be that couple that are living on the Charltons' ranch. That's where our cattle strayed awhile back, eh? Jack told me how mad you got, Mrs. Spencer. Well, come on in and sit."

This was more easily said than done, but our hostess managed to gather heaps of garments from the chairs and pitch them onto the tousled bunk beds. We sat down and I took stock of Maisie Jenner's home. We were in a large combination living room kitchen-cum-bedroom area, all of it untidy. Soiled dishes were piled on the one table and in the makeshift sink. Seeing my appraisal, Maisie apologized, after her own fashion. "Guess you caught us unawares, Jack will be right in and we'll eat, I'll put the coffee pot on, we never get up for breakfast here!"

Fascinated, I watched her toss out stale coffee grounds, and without any pretence of washing the pot, add fresh coffee and water. She placed this on the dirty top of her kitchen range to percolate. Then Maisie sloshed a small amount of cold water on top of some cups and plates in the dishpan and set them upside down on the table. She overheated a frying pan and threw in several chunks of unevenly-sliced pieces of venison. Soon cooking fat was spluttering onto the stove top and a pungent scorching smell permeated the room. I was horrified as I realized that I was actually going to be expected to eat this meal!

My husband apparently felt the same way I did, since he said, "We really don't wish to put you to any trouble, Mrs. Jenner, and we've practically promised Mrs. Hodges to go there for lunch. We just came to find out if you people have a milk cow you would sell to us?"

"It's no trouble at all!" Maisie asserted, "we won't let you run away so soon; we never get any company in this God-forsaken dump. As for selling you a cow, you can have the whole darned shooting-match for all we care!"

At this moment the master of the Lazy J Ranch entered. "What's all this about somebody wanting to buy my damned ranch?" he asked hopefully. He was as unkempt as his wife. Being unshaved added to his general shabby appearance, although it was the custom in the backwoods for men to wear beards. I could hardly believe Jack Jenner was only thirty-two years old, he looked close to fifty. He was somewhat flabby in spite of his occupation.

Arthur hastened to disillusion him. "Oh no, Jack! I don't have the money to buy a ranch or a herd, much as I'd like to be able to. We're starting on a shoestring, so I can only buy one milk cow if you have one for sale."

"Too bad! We'd sure like to get rid of this crummy ranch," said Jenner. "But we can sell a milk cow soon. Beauty is due to freshen in a couple of weeks, so in about a month you can have her."

"Very well, I'll take a look at her before we leave," my husband told him. I said I'd also like to see the cow. Buying one's first cow is a kind of milestone in a pioneer's life. I was not able to understand the Jenners' evident dislike of ranch life.

Then Maisie called, "Come and get it, folks. We don't go in for frills here, as you can see, but there's always lots to eat." We sat down to food which should have been a gourmet's delight, but this venison was scorched on the outside, underdone inside. I had watched the sloppy preparation and was almost afraid to eat or to drink the coffee. The men declared that it "hit the spot." The northern winters, it is true, give people a great appetite and most of the men in the backwoods were used to an uninspired cuisine, but I couldn't forgive my hostess' lackadaisical cooking and house-keeping methods.

The slaphappy meal did nothing to improve the Jenners' attitude towards life in the Cariboo and curiously I asked them, "What made you decide upon ranching if you find it such a tough deal? You say that until you came here to live you had never even been close to a farm or ranch. It seems an odd choice for such confirmed city people to make!"

"Heck! It was no choice of ours," Maisie scoffed, "Jack's Uncle Ben came to the Cariboo away back in the 1860's during the gold rush days and he struck it rich near Jack Of Clubs Lake. You'd think he'd had enough of roughing it after that and go back to the city and enjoy himself. But no! Darned if he didn't get hold of five hundred acres of wilderness and start cattle ranching."

Jenner continued the story. "Uncle Ben never married, he was actually my great-uncle and when he died he willed this ranch to my father. Dad was not well enough to live in the backwoods, so I was elected and we've lived here for ten years. Much too long as far as we're concerned. We'd sure like to unload the ranch!"

I'm willing to wager that if old Ben Jenner could have anticipated the kind of neglect that was in store for his well-planned ranch at the hands of his beneficiaries, he would have willed his property in a somewhat different way. Jack Jenner turned to his wife and said, "Better lend Mrs. Spencer your high rubber boots if she wants to go to the barn to see the cow."

"I don't think that will be necessary, I'll just step inside the barn and peek at her, I'm no judge of cattle, I'll leave that to Arthur," I remarked.

My hostess, however, produced the high boots and said suc-cinctly, "Better put them on, it's the only way you can walk in our barn as you'll see for yourself." I did as I was told and floundered along thigh-deep snow on the path that led to the barn, trying to step in places where the men's feet had been.

I hope I never see such a place again! Actually it was too dark inside to really see a thing, but I soon found myself slipping and wading in cow manure knee-high, with Maisie's boots threatening to remain behind each time I wanted to move forward. The odour was overpowering and this was not due to the presence of some ten cows in stages of pregnancy, but to the fact that manure had not been cleared from the barn floors for months. Arthur later remarked scornfully, "If that manure pile gets any higher, it will be easier for Jenner to build a new barn!" I got stuck finally and called into the odoriferous darkness, "Please bring a lantern. I need help!" What I really needed was a quick beeline out of there! My husband came and helped my progress through the muck, assisting me towards a stall where stood my former cow friend of the haystack rodeo affair. This then was Beauty, but now much more pregnant.

"There she is and you can have her for fifty bucks," said Jack Jenner. Arthur, who knew quite a lot about cows, having spent some time on a prairie farm where some cattle were kept, inspected the cow's udders and decided that Beauty should prove to be a good milk cow. Fifty dollars was all the cash we had until we received the next payment on our house in Vancouver. But for us a milk cow was a necessity and my husband arranged to come for the cow about a month later. The cow might miss her companions, I thought, but at least she would live in clean surroundings. I had to get out of that smelly barn as quickly as I could. Phew! Once outside I plunged into a clean white snowdrift to try and clean the boots. "What the heck are you doing there?" Jenner demanded.

"I'm trying to clean your wife's boots, I can hardly tramp into your house wearing them in this state!" I told him frostily. There was something about this man that never failed to bring out my worst qualities. I definitely must have been allergic to lazy cattlemen.

When I had put on my own boots again and bade farewell to the Lazy J, we rode back to the Hodges' ranch. Anne took one look at my face which must still have been registering the highest degree of disgust, and burst out laughing. "I can tell that you found the Lazy J! Isn't that place a disgrace, folks?"

"Disgrace is putting it mildly. The Jenners have no excuse, they are both young and with no family to look after! Here you are, Anne, a woman doing practically all the outside work alone and you have a model ranch with the best herds in the district!" I said emphatically.

"The difference between Maisie and me is that I love my family and our ranch home and the freedom of life in the Cariboo. She hates living away from the cities and doesn't mind airing her troubles. I hope they do sell as quickly as possible and move away from the district!"

After we had driven away from Hodges' ranch, Arthur decided to return to Deka Lake by the longer route so as to be able to stop and pick up any mail from the box on the main road which was more than a mile from Charlton's house. Along with several bundles of newspapers and letters from our parents there was also a letter postmarked Williams Lake. It was from Roy Charlton and said that they would be returning home in two weeks. They had gone directly to Roy's brother's home in order to get their team and sleigh which had been lent him shortly after our arrival at Deka Lake.

It was now the beginning of March and Arthur made two more trips up to Dragonfly Lake. We planned that when the Charltons arrived we would only have our beds and mattresses and blankets to carry up, along with canned or preserved foodstuff. My husband had been warned not to take any bedding before-time or pack rats would ruin everything. There was a huge population of these rodents and no one had been able to find any method of keeping them from invading human habitations in this wilderness of forests.

When he had informed me of this new pest, I was a little concerned. "Do you mean that pack rats are so bold that I shall have to practically make house pets of them? We'll simply have to devise some method of keeping them out of the house. One has to draw the line somewhere and my line is where the rats come indoors!" Actually, when I did see my first pack rats I found that with their bushy tails and custom of bringing something in exchange for the bright shiny objects that attracted them most in my home, that they did not seem like the ugly grey rats that invaded the garbage pails in cities. But we never became exactly chummy either, and I really had no need for small piles of stones or leaves which were their form of barter for hard-to-come-by nails and such things.

Our hosts arrived a week sooner than expected. They were still attired in city clothing and Mrs. Charlton gave the impression of being much more at home in a city office than in a backwoods cabin. Roy Charlton, however, was a dyed-in-the-wool rancher.

"Man, am I ever glad to get out of the crowded city and back here in God's own country again!" he assured us as he climbed down from the seat of the sleigh.

Arthur helped Roy unload a large amount of canned goods and stock feed. While the men took this portion of the load over to the barn, I helped Margaret Charlton store the groceries in her cupboards which I had hurriedly emptied of my things when they arrived. She first of all checked every item with a list she had in her purse. In her positive tones she said, "I hope you always thoroughly check *your* list whenever you buy from the general store in Lone Butte or from the mail-order houses. People are much more prone to cheat you than not!" How awful to have to be so mistrustful, I thought. Undoubtedly I was young and naive, but I felt her attitude towards other people, or perhaps her philosophy, was a hard one and not compatible with the wonderful peace of mind which we were able to enjoy in this beautiful land of Cariboo.

I saw Margaret looking at my bottles of preserved fish. "How did Arthur ever manage to find such a good spot? Roy has lived here most of his life and never been so lucky with a nightline!" she remarked a little enviously.

I explained how the trapper, English Deka, had stopped by and shown us how and where to fish through the ice successfully. As soon as I mentioned Deka, Mrs. Charlton looked at me with suspicion and said curtly, "Good heavens! I hope you didn't ask him to come inside? Those Indians can't be trusted. Why, they'd steal one blind if they got the chance!"

This seemed a good time to keep my own counsel; I wisely decided not to mention the women from the fishing camp whom I'd made welcome in this house. The camp was closed and the Indians gone back to Canim Lake, so I merely replied, "Don't you think that's too broad a statement? The Indians I've met so far have seemed decent and quite a lot like children in some ways. I've found them glad to learn something of our customs."

"Children indeed! Take my advice and leave them severely alone!" and she continued to grimly count her groceries. Plainly we were two different kinds of women, never likely to have much in common.

The departure time was soon upon us. We piled our belongings upon the sleigh, thanked the Charltons for their hospitality and drove away over the lake to our pre-emption on Dragonfly.

CHAPTER 12

Home on Dragonfly Lake

THE AFTERNOON SUNSHINE transformed the white expanse of Deka Lake into a diamond field and the air sparkled like wine. I was excited with the anticipation of starting life on land of our own. The future seemed full of promise. This was just my second trip to Dragonfly and as we approached the steep bank on which Johnny Winters' cabin stood, a man standing on the shore waved to us.

My husband waved back, saying, "That's Randy Jackson, he'll be our only really close neighbour and is looking forward to having people living nearby." When we came closer I saw that the man was in his sixties but broad-shouldered and possessed of a still youthful strength. He leaned forward to assist me from the sleigh and gave an amazed look at Roland bundled in blankets in my arms.

Smiling quizzically at Arthur he remarked, "You never mentioned that you were a father, young man. I'm not sure there'll be enough room in Winters' cabin after all; it's rather cramped, you know." Looking at me, he amended his words. "Well, she's just a little bit of a girl, so maybe she'll make do. I'll help you get started on a large new cabin, so your wife won't regret ever coming to the Isch-ka-bibble!"

Randy had already laid a fire in my big range and soon a cozy warmth filled the small one-roomed cabin. The men were unloading the sleigh and carrying our mattresses inside, along with Roland's crib and two large trunks full of clothing and household necessities. A big barrel of flour was rolled into a corner but there were still the preserved fruit and fish and groceries. The cabin measured just fifteen feet by twelve feet. In one corner I noticed a trap door, which I opened. I found that it led down three rough steps to a root cellar. All well-designed Cariboo cabins possessed these root cellars and they were an absolute necessity if one wanted to keep root vegetables and bottled foodstuffs from freezing and spoilage. Randy and Arthur carried our foods down and stored them on shelves set up for the purpose. With space at such a premium, I certainly was going to appreciate the root cellar.

While the men worked I did what was locally termed as "rustling some grub" and I presented the men with a meal which our new friend said was the best he had ever eaten. "When I'm with a family I realize what a poor lot a bachelor has. My cooking never was anything to write home about, but for that matter it's been so many years since I left my home in eastern Canada, that I've forgotten what the word really means."

"I hope then that you'll regard this as a second home, Randy, and I'm sure you'll be able to give us much helpful advice on how to live in the backwoods, we're just a couple of greenhorns, you know," I told our neighbour half jokingly, but with more truth than I could even dream of at the time.

When our friend had gone, my husband and I looked about us. Kitchen Queen occupied more than her fair share of the space, and a double bed, baby crib, trunks and boxes containing clothing, occupied every spare inch left in the small room. Arthur smiled, "There isn't room to swing a cat in here now!" It seemed as if both of us would soon be getting quite a lesson in togetherness.

Over the bed hung a horrible-looking bear skin, minus considerable portions of hair. "Do please take down that awful hide, dear, and put it outside. I certainly don't want that in the cabin." My husband looked dubious and muttered something about it meaning quite a lot to Johnny Winters, whose property it was. But I insisted, so the hide was removed, and, still muttering about women's whims, Arthur hung it upon the outside of the log wall. Satisfied, I hung a brilliant red Hudson Bay blanket in its place in order to shut out draughts caused by wintry winds that seeped through cracks between the logs where the moss packing had dried up and fallen out.

The piece de resistance of my interior decor was a large lithograph of one of Maxfield Parrish's paintings, depicting two lovely girls on a stylized gallery, overlooking the blue waters of Greece with a beautiful mountain background. When the rough type of living sometimes got me down, I would gaze at my picture and

in imagination travel far from the Cariboo to the sunny isles of Greece. This urge overtook me most often when the thermometer registered a grim sixty degrees below zero, a temperature which was decidedly new to my experience. I had grown up in the balmy air of Vancouver and the south coast of British Columbia. Finding foodstuffs, liquids in containers, bread, everything at all freezeable in fact, unusable each morning when I arose, was most disconcerting. Our drinking water had to be carried up the steep, slippery bank from the lake edge. For the many washings the baby required I brought in gigantic piles of fluffy snow and melted it on top of the stove.

By the end of March wild snowstorms were still frequent, and the lakes still icebound. Spring on this plateau, four thousand feet above sea level, was still six weeks or more away. I knew that in my former hometown, Vancouver, gardens were dappled with the gold of daffodils, pepped up with bright red japonica shrubs, and delicate strands of forsythia would be tracing patterns on the walls of bungalows. Rubbing cold hands together, I longed for the balmy airs of the south coast, then scolded myself for my lack of the real pioneer spirit. Still, despite my pep talks, I eagerly waited for the end of this long, long winter.

One morning the silence of the woods surrounding the cabin was broken by the sounds of voices and of jingling harness. A team pulling a sleigh stopped in front of our door and a man and a woman waved to us. Arthur went out to greet them and a lively, healthily plump woman climbed down from the seat and came towards me where I was standing in the doorway, not yet having put on my snowboots, so unable to step out onto the snowy path. The team was driven to the barn.

Almost before she reached me, the visitor was shouting excitedly, "I could hardly believe my ears when Eddie said we had new neighbours on Dragonfly, and that one of 'em was a woman!" I invited her inside, and barely catching her breath, the newcomer continued, "My, you've no idea how lonesome I've been nor how much I've longed for the sight of another woman. White woman I mean. But you're just a kid, ain't you? And your husband don't look no more than a boy himself. Eddie said he figured you was just a couple of kids, and darn it, he hit the nail right on the head!"

At that moment my ever-hungry son gave his feeding-time cry. My visitor looked amazed. "Don't tell me you've got a kid of your own, too." I picked Roland up out of his crib and proudly held him out for her inspection. "Heavens to Betsy!" she cried, "ain't that the cutest little baby. Imagine! A real honest-to-goodness family has come to live in the Isch-ka-bibble. I've been gettin' so fed up with just seein' men and Indian trappers!"

I wondered why Indian trappers did not come under the general heading of men, but still found that there was something sincere in this naive and talkative woman. I explained that we were more or less just camping in the Winters' cabin and that my husband would soon start to build a large cabin for ourselves.

"Sakes alive! I wouldn't care if you was holed up in a beaver lodge, just so's I had another woman for company. It's goin' to be handy for both of us. You can help me and I guess I can give you some pointers on livin' in the sticks, eh?"

"Oh, I'm sure you can be of great help to me, Mrs. Martin." Arthur had mentioned that Eddie Martin had a ranch further north.

My visitor gave an amused chuckle. "Just call me Jessie, dear. I'm not married to Eddie; I wish I was, but I'm just his housekeeper. I've got a miserable hunk of a husband livin' in Calgary, or did have! I dunno what's become of him since I walked out on him. Beatings and abuse from that man when he was drunk as a coot till I couldn't stand it another minute. So I up at last, and left him. I saw an ad in the Vancouver newspapers for a housekeeper and wrote about it. Eddie sent my fare and I came up here to work for him. I've been here for seven years and have never regretted it for a minute."

Jessie looked the picture of health and I told her that the pioneer life must certainly suit her. She appraised me in silence for a moment, then said, "Well, I think I could stand a beauty treatment. Hey! You're just the one to help me get on with my job of dyeing. I've been hankerin' to do it for months!"

Startled, I looked at my guest. It sounded as though she had said "dying." "You—did you say dying, Jessie?" I quavered.

"Yes, dearie! Hair-dyeing. I've been plannin' for ages to dye my hair a good red colour, but it's kinda hard to do this job right by myself. Now you're goin' to be livin' close-by, I can get some help with it. Think you could do a dye job?"

"Goodness, Jessie! I've never done anything like that, what if it turns out wrong?" I had unhappy visions of messing about with a pan of hair-dye and ruining not only my neighbour's hair, but a budding friendship at the same time. I remembered the story of

Anne of Green Gables in which the youthful heroine dyed a lovely head of red hair and came up with a horrible green effect. I told my new friend about my reservations but she wasn't in the least alarmed. She went on to explain in more detail why she wanted it done.

"You see, girlie, I've got a good man in Eddie and I don't want to lose him. He's miles ahead of that louse I was married to! Bein' a good cook and housekeeper ain't *all* there is to holdin' a man! I been readin' some magazines and they say a woman's got to keep on lookin' as young as she can. So I sent to one of these mail-order stores and got a packet of hair-dye and I aim to use it to get all prettied up for Eddie!"

How could I argue with such a philosophy? She won, hands down. I agreed to go up to the Martin ranch in the next few days and test my ability as an amateur hairdresser. But how I wished that I had never read about the story-book Anne's desperate plight. I succumbed, however, to Jessie's logic.

As I prepared lunch, my visitor chatted without ceasing, like a creek released by the spring thaw. It was quite evident that she was starved for the company of another woman. This was undoubtedly the country back of beyond, and seven years was a long time to be deprived of a chance to gossip with a member of one's own sex. Jessie was making up for lost time. I had already felt the loneliness of life in the Cariboo, so I understood her need.

Jessie's keen eyes roved about the room and paused upon the scarlet blanket occupying the wall where the grizzly hide had hung. "What happened to Johnny Winters' bear skin, girlie?" she enquired. I told her it was moth-eaten and no decoration any longer and that I had had it hung on the outside of the cabin.

"Johnny was mighty proud of that trophy. He said it could just as easily been his own hide as that grizzly's. Quite a story connected with the shooting of that particular beast." Of course this intrigued me immediately and I asked her to tell me about it.

"Well, I think everybody connected with this event got more thrills than they bargained for, but anyway, this is the way Johnny told it to us. John Winters was a pretty smart rancher and he had more cash in his jeans to start in cattle ranching than the average fellow. He came to the Cariboo from Texas and liked the country. Besides proving up on one hundred and sixty acres he leased an extra four hundred acres of range land, adjoining his pre-emption. He brought in good stock and was starting to make money. He had left his girl back in Texas and figured it was time he sent for her to come and get married. Lillian was her name and she was a pretty girl. She came up here with her married sister and brother-in-law. They could come only as far as Hodges' mailbox on the mail truck. From there on they had to ride horseback. Lillian's brother-in-law, Bob Smithers, had the biggest load of campin' gear you ever saw and it all had to be toted along, when Johnny met them.

"It came in handy though. Johnny turned over the cabin to the women and he bedded down with Bob in the tent. It was June and the mosquitoes was doin' their darndest to drive everyone mad. I rode down to visit a few days after they arrived, and my goodness! I laughed fit to kill to see the bed all hung about with white netting, just like a bride. But I couldn't blame those city folks at all because the bugs were driving me crazy too."

"Tell me! Are the mosquitoes really that bad in summer?" I asked my guest anxiously. The bites from these pests always poisoned my blood and gave me a particularly bad time.

"Yep, they're humdingers and that ain't all. There's the black flies, or some call 'em deer flies, almost as bad, and big horse flies. They raise cain with horses and cattle, but they bite humans too, they're not choosy. But Lillian and her sister soon had bigger troubles to upset them. At night all four of 'em could hear something splashin' about in that creek that runs back of the cabin, about two hundred feet away. Johnny told them it was a bear fishin' the creek. Bears stand in the water, get a wriggling fish in their paws and bat them out onto the bank. This one was mindin' his own business, havin' himself a whale of a time. But the women was nervous and started frettin' and worryin'. Couldn't Johnny just go out and shoot the bear and set their minds at rest?

"Poor Johnny! The women made such a fuss, he hadn't any choice. He told 'em the bear wouldn't hurt anyone and was never about in the daytime. Lillian was a stubborn little piece, so her sweetheart promised to sneak out after dark and shoot the bear.

"It was decided that both men go. They chose a dark, moonless night to hunt the bear. Johnny carried his .303 rifle, Bob had a light .22 calibre gun and a flashlight. Johnny told us it was so black they couldn't see six yards in front of them as they quietly crept towards the creek. The bear heard them, however, because the sounds of splashing in the creek waters stopped and everything became very still. Johnny's senses, too, were keen and he felt the presence of another creature close by. He whispered to Bob to shine the flash-light directly ahead of them. Bob did as he was told and there, right in front of them, was a huge bear reared up on his hind legs and all set to attack the unseen foe. Johnny yells, 'Shoot, man, shoot and run for your life!' He raised and aimed his rifle to where he thought the bear's head was, having seen it for just one instant. He fired and then turned and both men rushed for the cabin. Once inside, Johnny said they piled everything against the door, because even in that one short glimpse he knew that it was a grizzly and a wounded grizzly is about the worst foe in the world. Johnny did not mention *this* to the women but anxiously waited for what might happen should the bear follow. But nothing happened and they sat around drinking coffee until daylight came.

"In the morning the men cautiously crept back to the scene of the shooting. They had figured that the bear had been slightly hurt and made his escape in the darkness. But when they reached the spot what should they find but this great grizzly, dead as mutton! Johnny's chance shot had found the jugular and that lucky bullet had saved the men's lives!"

"Oh Jess, you tell a better bear story than English Deka and he told me some hair-raisers, too. But this one makes all his stories sound pretty tame. Killing a grizzly with one shot in the dark. Whee!"

"Listen, young woman," said my guest with some asperity, "those tales Deka tells are mostly a lot of baloney, but this one happens to be true. There's the bear hide to prove it besides the fact that Johnny wasn't alone when he shot the grizzly!"

"I'm sorry, Jessie! Really. I'm not trying to disparage your story, but it just seems so unbelievable, somehow! What did Lillian think of her sweetheart's courage and quick thinking?"

"Poor Johnny, he just couldn't win!" said Jessie. "It wasn't more than a week after he shot that bear before the visitors had packed their duds and gone and nothing settled about the wedding. Johnny was very disappointed, but he skinned the bear, tanned the hide and hung it on the wall of his cabin. He said it would teach him not to rush in where angels wouldn't or words to that effect."

"But didn't they get married, after all?" I asked incredulously.

"They did, but only on Lillian's terms," said Jessie disgustedly. "Two months after they returned to Texas, Johnny got a letter from his darlin' Lillian, sayin' he could choose between livin' alone in the Cariboo, or returning to Texas to marry her. Her daddy and her mummy would not consent to their daughter's having to go and live in northern Canada and maybe get chewed up by a hungry grizzly bear. Did you ever hear such crazy talk?" asked Jessie, her voice full of scorn.

"What a shame! Just when Johnny Winters was making such a success of cattle ranching, too! Talking of getting chewed up by grizzly bears, I think it might be a good plan for me to learn to use a rifle, don't you, Jessie?" I asked, remembering how many times I had put off getting started on mastering this vital skill.

"Good girl! Too bad Lillian didn't have some gumption herself! Anyway it meant that Johnny gave up ranchin' in this country. He sold his prize herd, Eddie bought up quite a lot of the cattle. Johnny closed his cabin door, said good-bye to us and went back to Texas. I do hope he and his scared little bride are livin' happy ever after," Jessie ended, a little acidly.

Arthur came in with Eddie Martin and it was evident that they were very congenial. We were four adults packed inside one cramped cabin, but Eddie was so entertaining that one could forget small discomforts. He seconded Jessie's invitation for us to visit them at his ranch within the week. He thought that the lake ice would soon break up and make it impossible to use our sleigh. Any travelling in summer and fall was done on horseback and at that time we didn't own one saddle horse. We had enjoyed meeting them and promised to return their visit.

CHAPTER 13

Arthur Saddlebreaks a Mustang

TWO DAYS LATER we drove the team up the narrow trail that led through snow-draped trees to Ed Martin's ranch on Drewry Lake in the Isch-ka-bibble country. On that brilliant late March morning there was a softening in the air, despite the fact that winter was still making a stand against the advances of spring, and the branches of jack pine and spruce were impatiently shrugging off their snowy blankets. In this pleasant isolation I found it hard to recall the hardships Arthur and I had undergone during the periods of unemployment in the city. It seemed far away and, as we reached Ed Martin's extensive and well-managed ranch, I gave silent thanks for our new-found peace out here in the wilderness.

One could see immediately that long hours and much effort had gone into building up this fine property. Large areas now covered with snow would, in season, be planted to feed crops. Ed Martin had bought John Winters' prize Hereford cattle and these were housed in warm, well-built barns. This rancher had purchased a Delco Light Unit which provided all the buildings with electricity, the first such system to be installed in this remote district of the Cariboo.

Electricity and its wonderful work-saving conveniences to me seemed little short of a miracle in this wilderness. The log cabin contained four large rooms and in the up-to-date kitchen Jessie was preparing a delicious-smelling lunch. She greeted us happily, "Good for you, you got here early. We'll have time to show you through the barns before we have lunch." The baby was left in the house, still sleeping cozily in his box, while we admired the cattle and a good-looking string of saddle horses.

"You wouldn't happen to have a spare saddle horse that you could sell me, Ed?" my husband enquired. "I'll need one when the spring break-up comes. I've already found out that I'll have a lot of work to do building a road before I can use the team."

Our host pointed to a large buckskin gelding. "That knothead, Arthur. If you can break him, he's yours for twenty bucks. I say 'if' because several fellows have tried and he's too darn ornery and I don't suppose you'll have any better luck with him."

Arthur, though, had had quite a lot of experience with horses on relatives' farms on the prairies. He claimed that he had a way with horses, so Ed Martin's offer was something like waving a red cape in front of a bull. A horse that couldn't be broken, eh? Arthur said he would have to see about that and there was no time like the present. He evidently felt a spell of bronco-busting coming on. "First of all I'll have to sack him out, Ed. Let's see how that works!"

"Sacking out" consists of rubbing gunny sacks about the horse's belly to accustom him to the feel of something against his body, and get him used to having a man handling him. The gelding took "sacking out" in his stride and did not even fuss when Ed slipped a halter about his neck while Arthur stood stroking the horse's nose and talking gently to him. But when my husband quickly placed a saddle on his back and securely fastened the cinch, the gelding tossed his head impatiently and immediately displayed temper when Arthur leaped into the saddle after leading the horse out of the barn.

I had never seen the breaking of a horse. The animal seemed to explode into the air, all his feet leaving the ground at once, but his rider hung on, just as full of determination as the horse. Then down plunged the forefeet, stabbing the snow-packed frozen ground of the corral. His rider was not unseated by this ruse, but crouched forward upon the horse's withers and hung on. The gelding appeared to think for a moment and then he commenced a dizzy whirl, a fast spin which combined speed with prodigious force. Ed Martin, watching the horse and rider with an incredulous grin, cried: "Watch that devil sunfishing, eh?"

Arthur was "acting nonchalant," but I was unabashedly scared, I expected to see him tossed violently to the ground at any minute, with several broken bones at the very least. That horse seemed extremely powerful. Apparently the gelding was getting annoyed by his rider's persistence and he decided to try another trick. He reared away up on his hind legs, up and up! My heart came up, too, and I had to stifle the scream lodged in my throat. I think I knew instinctively what would happen next, but so did my husband. I saw him yank his boots out of the stirrups, so that when the "ornery critter" (Ed's name for the horse) reeled completely over and fell heavily on his back in the trampled snow, his rider had become the man who wasn't there. Arthur had been one jump ahead of his mount the entire time and had slipped lithely from the saddle as the horse rolled backwards. After a vain attempt to remove the hated saddle, the horse got slowly to his feet and as he did so, my husband vaulted into the saddle.

"Your husband sure knows horses. I guess he knows how to break 'em, too," my host assured me, letting his eyes follow horse and rider as they began galloping about the corral. At the far end Arthur put his mount into a high jump which took them into a snow-covered pasture beyond. Horse and rider careened around this field in a mad gallop with my husband in full control. Gradually the horse sensed defeat and the gallop became a canter and then a sedate walk. Arthur put the gelding over the fence again and came in dignified fashion to where we watched.

My husband dismounted, spoke in friendly manner to the gasping animal and flung a blanket over the heaving sides as he led him into the barn. "Well, Ed, what do you say? He's the horse I want, we sort of clicked, finally. But right now I can't pay twenty bucks for him, our finances are scraping the bottom."

"Who said anything about cash?" asked Ed Martin amicably. "Suppose you give me a few days' work on my ranch. I've got an awful lot of fencing to put up. I need help a lot more than I need money." So the deal was made and Arthur was now owner of that spirited creature he had already named Speed.

We went back to the house and I found myself feasting on the most delicious food I had tasted since we arrived in the Cariboo. Jessie served us thick T-bone steaks of beef, snowy mashed potatoes, and stewed canned tomatoes. I had not enjoyed the latter for so long that I'm afraid I did more than justice to them. After we had left the Charltons' house where I had had plenty of root vegetables at my disposal, we had been unable to have this necessary food. We must wait until Arthur could ride out to Lone Butte for supplies. The lack of fruits and fresh vegetables was particularly distressing at this time as I was nursing my baby and required them more than at any other.

After lunch the men went out to decide where the fencing was to be done and Jessie promptly produced the packet of hair-dye and the necessary utensils for using it. "You won't have any trouble," she assured me confidently, "it tells you what to do, right on the packet!" I hoped she would prove correct. I had every intention of rigidly following instructions, but I still shrank inwardly from the task, remembering again the hapless Anne of Green Gables and her ruined tresses. Jessie chattered away happily, trusting her crowning glory to my most inexperienced hands. But luck was with me and the work went well and I was able to set the newly-tinted hair into a smooth wave.

We had to wait until Jessie's hair was dry and during the interval she told me many interesting tales of the people who lived in this lovely wilderness. Apart from the natives, these mainly consisted of bachelors, a few ranchers, and quite a number of men who made their living by trapping; so my hostess had lacked female acquaintances and was starved for the friendship of other women. When the hairdressing task was completed, both Jessie and I were agreeably surprised at the results. Jessie naively exulted, "Land sakes! Ed won't hardly know me, will he, dear? I don't believe a French hairdresser could have done any better. Maybe you should be operatin' a beauty parlour instead of bein' buried away up here in the sticks!"

While Jessie's hair was drying I had given her a facial treatment too, because like most pioneer women, she had little or no time for personal adornment. These backwoods women had so many chores indoors and out, to do every day, that it was easy to neglect the care of hair and complexion. To complete the transformation, Jessie exchanged her blue jeans and sweater for a more feminine dress. The men returned to the house at this time and Ed Martin stood still in utter amazement. "Whatever has happened to my Jessie? Well now, she's turned into one of those movie queens! What do you know?" Ed's pleasure was very evident.

Jessie preened herself in the general approval but said, "Don't be silly, Ed. A little hairdressing don't make that much difference. It's the same old me, underneath."

Giving me a mischievous grin, my husband had to say his piece, "Trust the 'little white mother' to start making changes here, too!" This called for explanations and my spouse told Jessie and Ed about my one-woman campaign to improve methods of child-training and hygiene amongst the Indians who had been at the fishing camp. Our host gave me an appraising look and remarked, "Well, Arthur, all I can say is that the change in Jessie's appearance is all to the good, and I've no doubt that the Indians also have good cause to be grateful to your wife."

We had declined the kind offer to remain for dinner as we did not know the trail to Dragonfly too well and wanted to return through the woods with daylight to aid us. Ed Martin started to assemble a box full of canned vegetables and fruits which he carried out and placed in the box of our sleigh. When we had put the baby in his warm little cradle beside these welcome additions to our menu, we thanked our hosts and drove away along the darkening trail. We managed to reach Winters' cabin before daylight was entirely spent. The tiny, crowded cabin was such a contrast to Martin's comfortable home that Arthur said, "I'll certainly have to get a move on and build us a good home, this is awfully pokey for three of us."

Arthur drove the team to the barn. Speed, our newest acquisition, had been tied behind the sleigh for the trip home. I think my husband spent considerable time at the barn admiring the beast and congratulating himself on finding this gem of a saddle horse. He remarked when he came indoors, "Johnny Winters left a quite good saddle hanging in the barn. It will suit me fine and when we get a payment sent from Vancouver, I'll mail Johnny the price of his saddle."

We knew that the break-up of ice on the lakes was due and Arthur decided that he must ride to Jenners' ranch and get the milk cow. Bringing her through thick brush would be very difficult.

CHAPTER 14

Danger Dodges Us as
the Ice Breaks Up

ARTHUR SADDLED SPEED early the next day and rode off across
Dragonfly where dark areas were beginning to appear, which Ed
Martin had told us marked a deterioration of the firm ice surface,
so that before long it could not be used to travel upon. "I'll make
good time getting to Jenners' place, but it may take some time to
lead the cow back, so don't look for me too early this evening," said
my husband before starting the trip.

I watched him ride away across Dragonfly towards the south
end from where a trail led through thick woods to Hathaway Lake.
As the day wore on a heavy March snowstorm developed and soon
I could scarcely see more than a few feet away from the cabin.
Everything became muted under a heavy fall of snow, but later I
heard the sound of horses approaching. I looked out to see that
two riders were dismounting and as they came to the cabin door I
recognized one of them as Danny Hatch, the father of the small
boy whom he had brought to me for help at Deka Lake.

Danny held out to me a large hindquarter of deer meat. "Is it for
me?" I asked doubtfully. I knew that the Indians had been without
meat just as we had during the long winter. "How did you know
where to find me?" I asked the young man.

"This first game of the season, Indian want to pay debt! I go to
Deka Lake house first. Little white mother him gone! Squaw with
bitter tongue say where you live. Danny bring meat to Dragonfly.
This Lily's man," he said, indicating his friend.

I suppressed a chuckle at the native description of the
unfriendly Mrs. Charlton. Apparently their dislike of each other

117

was mutual. "Will you come in and have hot coffee before you ride on? I'm very grateful to you for bringing me this meat." The visitors accepted my offer of coffee but left soon, saying they hoped to reach Canim Lake before it grew dark. They had had a successful first hunt and wanted to take meat to their tribe.

When my husband returned that night after his long ride, I would be able to set a delicious roast of venison before him. I divided the generous piece of meat and hung part of it in my small root cellar, safe from pack rats, and contentedly planned the evening meal which was to be such a welcome change from baked macaroni. Not that macaroni hadn't served us well, but one could get terribly tired of that old standby. I even thought up an eggless, milkless dessert as well. I began to anticipate a lovely celebration.

The afternoon brought an end to the snowstorm and the brilliant sunshine that followed made a white wonderland of the woods around Dragonfly Lake. It also accentuated the airholes in the lake, black watery patches showing in many places now. Arthur's plan to bring back the cow today had been a sensible one.

I had figured that my husband should be home by seven at the latest. But eight o'clock came and he was not back, I finally ate my dinner alone. The tasty roast was beginning to dry up and I was disappointed, but set Arthur's plate in the warming oven to try and keep things hot for when he got home. Roland had his evening bath and his meal and was put to bed. I tried in vain to read; my thoughts kept straying. Several times I stepped out onto the porch and peered towards the lake, but it was now a large indefinite area of blackness. I could see or hear nothing except the plaintive yapping of hungry coyotes far off. Suddenly, quite close to the cabin, the lonely howl of a wolf sounded and was answered by another howl further down the shores of the lake. Wolves! These would be the large black predators known as the Siberian or Russian wolf and a formidable foe.

I went indoors and really did some worrying. If the wolves were in a pack, they would not hesitate to attack a man. Arthur would be leading the cow and would not be progressing very fast. If there were only telephones in this country! But they were still several years into the future. Perhaps my husband had stopped overnight at the Hodges' ranch if he had seen that it had become too dark to continue the trip. With a telephone he could have contacted me and set my mind at rest. Pioneer women in this forbidding north country had often waited alone in some lonely cabin for husband or sons, and how often their men had never returned, victims of some mischance that had overtaken them in this tough, relentless land.

At midnight my vigil was still on, I couldn't dream of getting into bed and sleeping, I was far too tense. Waiting and listening! The night seemed endless, broken only by the baby needing his 2 a.m. meal. I had never been able to get him to forgo this feeding in the wee small hours, although the best hospitals recommend it. Suddenly my heart leaped; I heard Arthur give a command to Speed and approach the door. They were home at last! But my joy was shortlived.

Arthur sat down with a dejected slump of his shoulders and started to eat his dinner and drink the hot coffee I offered him. "I'm afraid our luck has run out, dear. That darned cow got as far as the lower end of Sulphurous Lake and simply refused to come across the ice. I just couldn't budge her an inch. I finally had to tie her up to a tree beside the lake and I've come back to try with the team and sleigh. I'll need your help, too. Our best plan will be to get the cow onto the sleigh and haul her home. We must get back right away, I heard that wolves are running in packs, so that fool cow would be just like a sitting duck if the wolves spot her there!"

"But what about Roland? I can't leave him here alone! I guess I'd better wrap him up warmly and put his little box in the sleigh, don't you agree, Arthur?"

"No, I don't agree! This is no place for a five-month-old baby. We'll have that cow in the sleigh if we can get her in. Our child will be much safer here. I hope we won't be away for very long." My husband went to the barn to harness the team and I fussed around like an old hen, putting the fire in the stove completely out and blowing out the coal-oil lamps. I knew that I'd worry about my son, he had never been left alone in his life, but now circumstances demanded that I leave him here in this isolated cabin while I went out at three o'clock in the morning to try and help bring back a balky cow over the weakening surface of the lake ice. I never could have anticipated having to make such a choice. The north country was a hard taskmaster.

I joined my husband on the seat of the sleigh. He had tied Speed on behind just in case, he told me, we might need the saddle horse, too. The melancholy howl of the wolves sounded again, quite nearby. The frightening ululations echoed from hill to hill around the lake. Arthur told me he had stopped for lunch with the Hodges as he didn't want to have to eat another meal with the Jenners. Anne Hodges had told him that the wolves had been seen on Sulphurous Lake in groups of seven or eight.

The waning moon made the scene as bright as day and it also revealed to my startled eyes the number and extent of the airholes. They looked larger and far more dangerous than viewing them from the safety of the shore. "Good heavens, Arthur!" I exclaimed nervously, "do you think it's wise to bring the team and sleigh out on this rotting surface. It looks awfully risky to me!"

My husband was exhorting the team to the best pace they were capable of. "Giddap Molly. Shake the lead out of your feet, Daisy!" Turning to me he said, "I had no alternative really. We need that cow, and when I paid Jack Jenner, it took the last of our cash. Knowing these wolves are around, I feel we *must* take the chance! I'm sure she wouldn't be there in the morning."

Often the large hoofs of the team seemed to barely miss a huge hole where the water spread out on the top of the ice, but my husband guided the horses with a sure hand and we were soon on the short portage between Dragonfly and Hathaway Lake. This lake being longer required more time to traverse, but finally we reached Sulphurous Lake and here the holes seemed even larger and more numerous. I admit that my imagination works overtime in cases like these and once I barely repressed a frightened scream. "Relax, dear! You're too tensed up, everything is going fine! Before long we'll be down to the place where I've tied the cow," my husband said, reassuringly. He seemed to have nerves of steel.

We passed the Hodges' house all in darkness. It was about three-thirty and intensely cold, although I felt hot with excitement. Arthur was gazing intently down the lake and I stared too. Did I really see five black forms rapidly crossing the ice, or was that, too, a figment of my imagination? But my husband said, grimly, "Yes, you really see wolves, I'm afraid we'll be just a few moments too late. Shout! Yell! Make all the noise you can. Giddap, Molly, Daisy!" He brought the whip down smartly on the horses' rumps. Startled by such unaccustomed severity, the team put their backs into it and we sped down the final piece of lake ice as if the devil were after us, instead of in front, in the form of five huge and hungry Siberian wolves.

Yelling like banshees, we converged upon the spot where the cow loomed, a black blur near the lake edge. Almost at the same time the wolves completed their run across the lake from its western shore. The noisy arrival of the team and drivers deterred them temporarily, as they slunk into the cover of shrubs at the shore. My husband jumped off the sleigh seat and reached behind into the box and brought out his rifle. He took random aim and fired in the general direction the wolves had run. Apparently he found a target because a high howl filled the night, followed by a violent thrashing in the brush and then such a savage snarling and the heart-stopping noise of crunching fangs on bones! One of the wolves had been shot and was now being attacked by his companions. I shuddered as I turned my attention back to the cow.

She regarded us with suspicion. Now what did we think we were going to try to make her do? Arthur placed the gun in the sleigh box and removed from it a large door which he set at the back of the sleigh. He untied the cow and led her to the make-shift ramp and tried to lead her up this, but the heavy animal pulled back on the rope and braced herself for a struggle. It was a ridiculous sight, no doubt, a man and woman shoving and pulling at that stubborn creature, but we were desperate and kept trying for an hour. What a mistrustful bovine! In the brush the yellow glow of the wolves' eyes reminded us that they were just waiting for a chance to rush upon us. Finally, exasperated, my mate gave up. "It's no use," he said, replacing the barn door on the sleigh. "Do you think you could ride herd upon this cow, if I tied her to the back of the sleigh, sort of keep her walking straight alongside? It seems to be about the only means to budge her!"

I looked at Speed, remembering that he was just recently saddlebroken. I specifically recalled the many devious ways he had devised to unseat his rider. Nevertheless, with a do or die attitude, I told my husband that I was willing to try this plan. So he untied Speed and put the cow in back of the sleigh. I mounted the horse and Arthur took the reins, and the team, glad to be in motion again, started back up the lake.

For a short time all went well, I even forgot to search for large airholes. I felt leery of Speed, however, and in the uncanny way of animals he sensed my fear. In spite of having been warned not to display fear of animals since I had come into the wilderness, the feeling was there and I couldn't hide it. Perhaps the tense way in which I grasped the neck rein informed my mount, because soon he began to shove closely against the side of the sleigh, so that my leg was being jammed against it. Or else he shoved against the flank of the cow which was worse. Up until now she had been going along with the idea, but Speed's ornery actions put a stop to that and the cow started to pull back on her rope.

Arthur shouted back over his shoulder asking what was the trouble. I told him and suggested that we change places. I had driven the team a few times and, anyway, I wouldn't mind giving up riding Speed who appeared to be a completely one-man nag. So we made the change and things went along as before Speed started his shenanigans, except that I tensely peered ahead and gasped at every large airhole as we came up to it. "Stop worrying, the horses don't want to walk into a hole any more than you do!" said Arthur, sympathetic to my fear although not comprehending it.

How wonderful it must be to have so much faith in the horses; I wished that some of this confidence would rub off on me and I admired my mate even more than I ever had before, but I went on fighting to keep my heart where it belonged and not up in my throat! We covered Sulphurous Lake, Hathaway, and made the portage over to our own lake, Dragonfly, without any mishaps and I began to feel that my fears had been unfounded.

Only three miles to go! I relaxed and that made everything so much worse when what I feared, actually did happen. About half-way across Dragonfly there was a tremendous cr-r-ack! The ice suddenly split right beneath the runners of the sleigh and huge jagged fissures shot out in all directions. The team drew to a standstill, casting terrified glances back towards us. Did the ice actually heave and tilt beneath us? It certainly seemed to! Here, just a mile from safety would we all plunge to our deaths in the icy waters? I prayed wildly and stifled my screams and heard Arthur yelling urgently at me, "Keep the team going! Don't let them stop or we'll all be killed! Giddap Molly, Daisy, giddap there!"

In her terror, all her original fears about travelling on ice having been confirmed, that nerve-ridden cow had slumped forward on her knees and was bawling to the skies! Arthur rode his horse forward, pulling the cow to her feet. The team responded gallantly as I applied the whip; they realized the danger as much as we did, and stepping carefully, they started away from the dangerous spot and the ever-widening area of dark water. Gingerly the horses drew the sleigh onto safer ice. Arthur had managed to calm the cow enough so that she plodded behind and we covered the remaining distance to the safety of the shore. I said a heart-felt prayer when we finally climbed off the ice to the bank. I can't remember ever being so happy to feel solid ground beneath my feet! With a relieved sigh I jumped from the sleigh and dashed towards the cabin while Arthur drove the weary horses and frightened cow to the welcome shelter of the barn.

I ran into the cabin to find that the baby was still peacefully sleeping although the cabin had grown very cold. I hastily lit the fire in the range and prepared coffee and a hot breakfast for my husband. He never needed sustenance more, I'm positive. When he came indoors the first thing he did was to hold me tightly in his arms. "I'd never have managed to get that cow home unless you had been there to help," he declared gratefully.

"I don't think I was of much help," I replied, "we seem to be learning to pioneer the hard way, though I doubt if there ever was an easy way. I guess it's all in the day's work as Jack Jenner would say. But I hope it's not all going to be as tough as this night has been. Still we proved we can stand on our own feet, and I think we earned a promotion from the tenderfoot status!"

Our real help came from God, who surely and safely guided us out of danger that night and before we slept we both acknowledged our debt to the Creator of all things on earth.

CHAPTER 15

Spring Comes to Dragonfly

OUR NEW COW REQUIRED a few days to recuperate from her ordeal on the lake ice but after that she proved to be a prolific milker. I searched through my recipe books to find desserts or casserole dishes that would use great quantities of milk. I set out flat, shallow pans and skimmed off the cream for making butter. I had brought a small churn with me for this purpose, but I did not have the type of thermometer that would determine the temperature of the cream when it was ready for churning. I had been told that it should be at room temperature, but in Winters' cabin that varied so much that I could only guess at what was correct. Often I guessed wrongly and I would sit there fruitlessly turning the handle of the small churn, burning with impatience when the milky fluid refused to become little beads and clots of butter.

But perseverance paid off in the end and I did produce butter. Then there was the task of washing every trace of buttermilk out, and how I longed for the running water from a faucet. I was obliged to use water obtained the hard way, dipped from the lake and carried in pails up the steep and slippery bank to the cabin. Beauty was still being fed the wild hay Arthur had bought from Roy Charlton and hauled by sleigh up the length of Deka Lake to Dragonfly. Her milk was not as rich as it would be when she went out onto fresh pasture, so I had to add some colouring to the butter at first, but was able to discontinue this when summer returned to the Cariboo and the lush meadows made living easy for the herds of cattle and strings of horses. It was also the reason that game returned in large numbers to this fertile plateau in the heart of British Columbia.

Late in April, we awakened one day to the sound of a high soughing in the tree tops. We went outside to find that there was a strong, warm wind moving across the land and the water. "It must be a Chinook. I wasn't sure if they had them in this province, but it certainly seems like a Chinook and the lake ice will go very quickly," my husband informed me. Since our return with the cow the lake surface had been unsafe for travel. Large brownish areas of water had appeared on top of the ice, giving it a dirty and spongy appearance.

The heat from the sun increased as we watched big cakes of ice moving towards the small river that drained Dragonfly. Our heavy winter clothing grew unbearably warm and we began peeling off sweaters and coats. My small son also was becoming uncomfortable and I removed some layers of knitted woollens from him, too. "Isn't this glorious?" I rejoiced, "it feels like summer. Look at the ice jam at the end of the lake!"

A subdued roaring sound came from that direction, the ice was really piling up in the narrow outlet from lake to river. An increase in the roar informed us that the ice jam was being attacked by the warm but forceful wind. The grey chunks of ice dissolved and soon disappeared in the rushing water of the river, leaving behind a blue, glittering expanse of lake that reflected a sky full of white scudding clouds.

The same wonderful change was taking place on shore. Drifts of snow which had slowly been shrinking during the past month, suddenly were gone. Numerous tinkling little rivulets escaped over the brown earth, filling the air with a fairy-like music. I felt as if I had just entered a new country, one teeming with signs of life instead of frozen with winter's deadness. I never welcomed spring so wholeheartedly in all my life as I did that first one on Dragonfly Lake.

As if they had received some signal, which was probably the case, birds returned to the Cariboo in great fluttering, song-filled numbers, having spent the winter in the more hospitable south. It is true that the Canada jays and cheery little chick-a-dees had stayed with us all winter long because I had fed great numbers of them both at Deka Lake and on Dragonfly, and they had become extremely tame and very dependent upon me. I had been able to stand still and have them alight upon my shoulders and the saucy whiskey-jacks, as we called this species of jay, were so tame that often they became quite a nuisance.

With the advent of spring came the flickers, agile colourful members of the woodpecker family, and their cousins the red-crested woodpeckers, nifty in suits of contrasting black and white presenting a most elegant appearance, although they were most useful members of the bird kingdom. The woods began to resound with a multitude of hammerings, as if a colony of carpenters had commenced a building project. Arthur and I could never stop marvelling over the perfectly round hole the flickers would drill in a cottonwood tree, preparatory to scooping out the space inside to make their nests. No set of compasses ever made a truer circle.

We saw our first mountain bluebirds sensibly taking over a last year's flicker nest which had been discarded for a new model this spring. For sheer beauty of colouring I thought that nothing could compare with the rich bright blue plumage of the male mountain bluebird. The more attractive colouring applied to all the male bird kingdom, of course; the hens had work to do! They were much too occupied with the serious business of mating, nest building and the hatching of eggs and raising of chicks. They didn't have time to worry about fine feathers!

But there were also the predators. We often saw a baldheaded eagle hunched upon the bare branch of a lightning-blasted jack pine, watching keenly for the chance to swoop and make a killing among smaller birds or mammals.

Hawks of many kinds were prevalent in these north woods and ducks that fed in the reedy little bays of the lake came in so many varieties that I can't remember the names. When darkness fell, the mournful hoot of owls filled the night. There were small types like the Screech Owl and the larger Horned Owl, much feared by smaller birds, small rodents, frogs and lizards. The crows and ravens managed, as a rule, to keep the great Horned Owl in his proper place by using the strategy of numbers; they ganged up on him, in short. But once in a while the owl took his revenge, as a heap of shiny black feathers would attest, all that was left of an unlucky crow after the owl had found his dinner.

Arthur remembered a case where a great Horned Owl had, without provocation, attacked a young lad who was drawing water from a well on the family ranch. The boy did what he could to protect himself from the clawing talons and thumping strong wings, but was left blinded by the owl's unexpected attack. Generally speaking, however, owls shun close contact with men despite their nightly question, "Who? Who?"

But the bird that really spelled Cariboo to me was the loon. Almost as soon as the ice went out of the lake I heard the most eerie cry. It was desolate, yet it held a curious independent undertone, as if it really was not at all concerned about man and his pursuits. He still possessed his lonely lakes in the north woods. I had never heard this odd bird cry before on the south coast and asked what it was.

My husband, looking across the still water, told me, "That is a loon. You've heard the saying, 'Crazy as a loon' haven't you? He sure does sound crazy doesn't he?" But I didn't think so. The yodelling cry had a haunting quality, speaking to me of lonely lakes where men had not yet gone. Later, when we had built a small boat for getting about on the lake to fish, I was able to examine loons at close quarters because they would come right alongside the boat, eyeing me fearlessly from their comically red-circled eyes that made them look like clowns. They do not fear men, perhaps because it is illegal to kill loons. It was almost as if these favoured creatures knew in some uncanny way that the government had them under its wing. Loons wore neat black and white speckled suits and were the most ardent fishermen.

When I went out to fish I usually would row and row about with two rods extended over the stern, and quite often not have the least bit of luck at catching a trout for dinner. Then I would see a loon dive in almost under my boat and come up with a tasty-looking trout wiggling in his beak. I didn't exactly grudge the loon his fishing prowess, just wished that mine were a little better. He would yodel forth his triumph as I dejectedly rowed to shore and carried home an empty creel. There were just one pair of loons that lived on Dragonfly Lake and one of the old-timers in the country told me that it seemed to be the way the loons arranged matters, one pair pre-empted the waters of one lake. I imagine Deka Lake, being a long and fairly wide body of water, could accommodate more than two loons, however.

One morning Arthur called me out to a meadow where I noticed the faintest mist of green that tinted the brown earth. "Come here and stay perfectly still. Did you ever hear grass grow?" he asked me. I listened carefully, almost holding my breath, and I positively did hear tiny clicks, even though to most ears they would have been inaudible. Each minute click, my husband assured me, signaled a tiny bit more growth on a blade of grass. In the great silence of the Canadian north, spring's phenomenal growth could actually be measured in sound.

During the month of June the flowers also bloomed in great haste as if they had been detained too long by winter's straitjacket. It was as though Nature tried to compensate for such a late spring by prodigally spilling her wealth of blossoms in that one month of riotous colour. First I found pale mauve and faintly gold dog-tooth violets and the lovely russet columbine, graceful as a ballet dancer in the woods; and then pink, clover-like blooms which cattle gorged upon and the poisonous blue lupine which the livestock shunned. Brilliant red Indian paint-brush, the roots of which had been used for making dyes by the natives for generations, made spots of vivid colour everywhere and yellow daisies studded the meadows, while blossoms on all the berry bushes informed me where I should find fruits later in the year.

All was not idyllic, however. With the pleasant warmth came myriads of huge mosquitoes which soon became the bane of my existence. These king-sized pests stung me and poisoned my blood, and the many scratches soon became infected. My small son suffered in the same way, and my helplessness to prevent injury to his sensitive baby skin made matters even worse. There was no screen on the one small window or the door. Arthur, who soon developed an immunity to the pests, advised making smudges in the cabin. I was ready to try anything! We filled empty cans with wet leaves after getting a few dry slivers of wood burning. These made smudges with a capital S and almost blinded us in the bargain. But they did nothing to lessen the attacks of the ravenous mosquitoes. We finally discovered that the insects were actually hatching beneath the shake floor of the cabin and merely flew up from beneath the cracks in this rough floor, so we were defeated before we even began to fight.

One morning I blinked through the blue choking smoke to see our neighbour, Randy Jackson, standing in the doorway. "What in creation is going on here, folks?" he gasped, "you'll choke to death, all of you!"

"Mosquitoes! They're driving me crazy! These smudges are supposed to keep them out, but they're not helping one bit!" he was told between coughs. He looked commiseratingly at Roland who was crying in discomfort. "I know of something that may be helpful. The natives make a salve of herbs and a certain clay, but won't tell me what it is. But I will get some from them and let you try it!" Randy promised.

He was as good as his word and two days later came again with this salve. I applied it liberally to the baby's skin and to my own. It was a bluish-grey mixture and nobody could have recognized me, but it did lessen my appeal to the voracious pests.

Then came the black flies, known locally as deer flies. This variety of pests could and did remove pieces of flesh from their victims, either man or beast, almost as large as themselves. I would come in from a short period out-of-doors, bleeding profusely, looking as if I had tangled with a bear. As if these weren't scourge enough, we had great horseflies which made life a hell for horses and cattle. At this time no sprays had been developed for ridding one's stock of these irritating pests and the teams used by ranchers were very hard to handle for this reason. If a person went swimming in the lake he was most ardently welcomed by horseflies. I can never forget their vicious attacks whenever I tried to indulge in my favourite hobby of swimming.

"We've got more trouble," announced Arthur one morning as he set down the pail of milk. "Speed, Molly and Daisy are simply crawling with ticks! We'll have to get busy on that next."

"Ticks!" I screeched. I thought I had already encountered every type of stinging or crawling insect known to man. "What kind of ticks do you mean?"

"Randy warned me about these grouse ticks. The animals brush against the bushes now that they are out on pasture and that's where they pick up the ticks. They thrive just as well on livestock as on wild birds, apparently. I have a wash here with a strong creosote base and we're going to have to scrub the horses with this to kill the ticks. Do you think you could help me?"

No task could have pleased me less, but I was wife to a pioneer rancher, wasn't I? So I gamely offered my services. "I think I can help scrub Molly and Daisy, but Speed is a horse of a different colour!" I told my husband.

The remainder of that beautiful spring day was spent dealing with ticks and we didn't spare the creosote wash. When Arthur said that the horses were crawling with ticks he was not exaggerating! They were a loathsome grey mass all over the bellies and hindquarters of our horses. Luckily the animals co-operated one hundred percent as we worked on them. Even Speed, that high-spirited beast, stood quietly as I sloshed the mixture on his hide and Arthur scrubbed with a curry brush. He was all for having us rid him of those awful blood-sucking insects.

When the task was done I felt terribly crawly and dirty myself. "The water in the lake may not be warm enough for bathing but this is one time when the space in our little tub won't hold enough water for me to come clean. I'm for the cool, cool lake!" I cried, and raced down the slope and let the lovely, invigorating depths of Dragonfly receive my body. Half an hour later, cool, refreshed and clean, I felt I was back to normal. I might add that removing ticks from the hides of animals is not exactly my idea of a pleasant pastime, but like many others which had to be done from time to time, it was part of getting a start at ranching amidst pioneer conditions.

The following day Ed Martin and Jessie rode out of the woods and greeted us laughingly, "Oh, you're still here! Randy told us what a tough time you were having with the mosquitoes! We wondered if they'd driven you out of the Isch-ka-bibble?"

"They're doing their best, Jessie!" I told her, "but this salve that the natives make seems to help a great deal. Randy was kind enough to bring me some. When I put this clay on I feel as if all I need is a feathered bonnet to enable me to play the part of Sitting Bull's squaw. But gradually we are getting used to these pests. How are things up at the ranch?"

Jessie answered that was what had brought them to Dragonfly today. But Ed would be talking to Arthur about the matter. We strolled about and Jessie bent down and picked some little growths which she explained were morels, a type of edible mushroom. They were numerous, and my guest said were fine for pepping up venison or moosemeat steaks and other dishes. "I'm glad to know about them because I've seen plenty of them in the woods. Arthur has been busy cutting down trees and swamping out a road down the west side of Dragonfly so that he can drive his team out and get to town for supplies. We can't bring in much of a load of groceries on a saddle," I explained as we chatted.

"If you run short of anything, be sure to let me know," Jessie offered generously. "Ed just about buys out the store when he drives into Lone Butte, so we have plenty of everything."

I was thankful that I still had several bottles of canned trout on hand and was able to serve my guests a good meal. Then Arthur asked casually, "Do you think you could manage here at the cabin alone during the week, dear? Ed needs a full-time hired hand and has offered me the job for the season. But I won't leave you if you're afraid to stay alone."

Not for the world would I have let my friends know that I was just as frightened of the woods and wild animals as when we arrived, five months before. I was a tenderfoot in the wilderness and didn't pretend to be anything else. But I was also practical and knew that the small sum of money that came to us from the purchasers of our house in Vancouver was just enough to buy necessary groceries and would not purchase any livestock for starting a ranch. If Arthur went to work for Ed Martin our plans for building a larger and better cabin would have to be postponed and I dreaded another long winter in such a crowded, tiny space. But I decided that if this is what my husband thought was best I was ready to go along with it. I assured them that I wasn't at all afraid to stay alone on Dragonfly.

"I'll ride home every Saturday evening, of course," my husband said. "Naturally I'll want to know everything is okay here and make sure you have firewood. Do you think you could milk the cow?" he asked. I said I could. I had often milked her when Arthur had other chores to do or was working on the road he was making. I had also carried pails of water up the steep bank from the lake, so felt quite self-sufficient, as a pioneering wife should.

But after we said good-bye on Monday morning and I had watched him ride into the dense woods in the direction of Drewry Lake where the Martin ranch was located, I did not feel quite so chipper. With just a tiny baby still too young to talk, for company, it was going to be darned lonesome! When I could no longer hear the horse's movements on the trail, I knew that I was now entirely on my own.

I was now accustomed to and listened eagerly for the yodelling of the loons on the lake, the screech of eagles and of hawks and the other sounds of birds in the woods. What did scare me was rustlings and the crack of fallen branches that to me denoted some larger species of fauna. What was that? I would ask, startled when standing beside the lake to hear some unexpectedly loud noise that came from the thick underbrush back of Winters' cabin. I would dash back because my son was sleeping there, then wait, listening tensely for whatever had made the sound to appear. Would an immense grizzly wander out into the clearing and find me defenceless and at its mercy? Were those great Siberian wolves still in the vicinity? If there was anything at all that I could dream up in the way of four-footed predators, I conjured them right in front of that lonely cabin.

My jitters grew worse rather than better and I knew that I must overcome my fears somehow. I had it! I would learn to shoot. Every backwoods woman should be able to use a rifle. I had to lift myself out of the tenderfoot class by my own volition. Nobody else could do it for me. Gingerly, I raised the heavy rifle from the rack beside the door and learned to swing it up to my shoulder and hold it firmly in that position. It was far too heavy a gun for me, but just sighting through the sights—even though I didn't actually fire it at first—gave me a feeling of confidence that I certainly needed. I began to feel that should I be attacked I could use the gun at a pinch. My practice with the rifle had most value as a morale builder, I believe, because I certainly did gain a feeling of security.

CHAPTER 16

Living and Learning
in the Northwoods

THE FIRST WEEK that I was alone at Dragonfly, I did not venture far afield; I managed to get as far as the barn and back twice daily to milk the cow, and went down the sloped bank to the lake to carry up water. But when nothing untoward happened, I plucked up courage and carried Roland down to the shore and laid him there wrapped in a cocoon of blankets, while I waded in the cool waters. This was tantalizing as I love to really swim, so the following day I placed my son in one of the native carrying cradles which my friend, English Deka, had obtained for me, and fastened it securely against the trunk of a sapling. This enabled me to have some swimming close to the shore where I could also watch the baby or hear him should he cry.

One afternoon I was standing near the barn and sighting at an improvised target with the heavy rifle, when a man's voice suddenly startled me out of a year's growth. "Don't shoot, lady! I'll come quietly." It was our friend the trapper, Randy Jackson. He had crept so silently out of the woods wearing native moccasins on his feet, that I had not heard so much as a snapped twig. Long years of travelling in brush country made it possible for him to move without making a sound, so I was taken completely by surprise. In some consternation I hurriedly put down the rifle and Randy laughed and looked pointedly at the pail of milk beside the path.

"Don't tell me you have to hold a gun on that cow to get some milk from her, young lady," he teased as he picked up the gun. "You're not holding this rifle the right way. You must hold it up tight against your shoulder, these guns have quite a kick back when they're fired. You need a few lessons, I can see."

"You're quite right, I must learn how to shoot this rifle, I'm nervous here alone. I keep imagining that all kinds of wild animals are about to swoop down on me and the baby, Randy."

"Here alone, girlie? Where's your husband? Seems to me he shouldn't leave a trigger-happy young woman fresh from the city alone here to run the show. Gee! I'd sure hate to be the first bear that poked his nose out of the bush!" said my visitor.

We went into the cabin and Randy looked longingly at the fresh milk. "It's been so long since I drank good fresh milk I think I could drink a whole pailful. That's one thing I really do miss in my bachelor paradise," he said whimsically.

I filled a large pitcher and set it before him. "Drink all you want, Randy. Beauty gives so much milk I can't possibly find a use for all of it. Arthur has gone to work full time for Ed Martin and just gets home for Saturday evenings and Sunday. He had intended to make a cheese-press for me but there are so many chores he has to catch up on Sunday, that he hasn't had time."

The old man thoughtfully consumed a quart or so of milk. He picked my son up out of his crib and handled him fondly on his knee. "Do you know, girlie, I've been missing the best things in life, and that's a good wife and family of my own. Things just did not work out that way for me. Still, maybe it's not too late for me to get a ready-made family. What do you say, girlie? Do you think we could work something out between us? I believe I could be of help to you young folks right now. The fact is, I don't think you should be alone here, this is a pretty isolated spot. Why don't I just tote my bedroll over here and bed down in the barn loft? My saddle horses can run with yours and I could get a lot of work done here, and in return I would have my meals with you and enjoy some company which I'm sadly in need of. How does that appeal to you?"

To say that I was pleased with the old trapper's suggestion was putting it mildly. "It would be marvellous, Randy. If you're sure it won't interfere with your own work? There are so many chores that require a man around the place that never get done since Arthur started working for Ed Martin on his ranch."

"Indeed no, trapping is finished for the season. I had promised to help your husband build a big new log house this summer, and living here would make things easier all round. I can start picking out the logs, get them cut, peeled and hauled, ready to put them up as soon as Arthur is through working at Drewry Lake." Before my husband returned for his weekend visit, Randy was already installed as boarder and had started cutting logs for our icehouse.

Arthur was very happy about the new arrangements as he had been worried about leaving me alone on Dragonfly all through the week. "Say, this is very good of you, Randy," he told our friend, "I'll work better and sleep easier, knowing you're here to keep an eye on my wife and son. I sure hated the idea of leaving them here, and Olive won't admit she's frightened of wild animals and all sorts of imaginary creatures. She tells me that you're teaching her how to use a rifle?"

Randy laughed and explained how I had swung the rifle upon him and covered his approach. "A little knowledge could be a dangerous thing and she might have hurt herself a lot more than she could have hurt whatever she was aiming at, but she's catching on fast, son! Say, there's something we sure could get a lot of use out of if we had one and that's a small skiff. D'you know anything about boat-building?"

My husband was very proficient at carpentry work and they tackled the problem of building a boat from which we could fish and thus bring more variety to our menu. They searched John Winters' barn but could not find the right material for making a skiff. "I guess that means a trip to town to get lumber before we can do a thing," said Arthur, disappointed at such a delay.

Randy was not stumped, however. "Get the team in, son, and hitch them up to that old wagon of Johnny's behind the barn. I've got some boards at my cabin which I believe will be just right. I don't think I'll be wanting to use them anyway." My husband found Molly and Daisy and soon the men had gone over to Randy's homestead. They returned with the necessary material and made good progress. Arthur, by taking over all available space in the cabin, managed to produce a steam bath out of my copper-bottomed boiler and steamed the ends of some boards to form the bows of the little skiff, no mean feat in itself when one considers the space he had to work in. By the time it was dark, all that remained to be done was the caulking. Randy had found what was needed for this in Winters' barn. "I remember he was going to build himself a boat, he told me he had been fishing from the banks and not getting nearly the catch that he would if he only had a boat. But it seems doubtful that Johnny will ever be back, so we'll make use of this material and it won't be wasted," the old man decided.

On Monday morning as Arthur was riding away to Martin's ranch he said, "Dig up all your cheese recipes, Olive. I have the cheese-press just about finished. I've been working on it in the evenings and will bring it home next Saturday."

"Wonderful! I've hated wasting all the extra milk we now have to spare," I said as I gave my husband a grateful smile. When I found my cheese-making recipes I discovered that I would need an ingredient just as necessary as the milk itself and that was essence of rennet. Randy had heard that Ralph Hodges was going to Lone Butte for supplies, so he saddled his horse and rode down to Sulphurous Lake with a list of groceries for us which included the rennet. But when he returned a couple of days later Pa Hodges informed him that the storekeeper not only did not have rennet, he had never heard of it. So Ralph had thoughtfully added this article to a list which Anne Hodges was mailing to Eaton's Mail Order Store in Winnipeg.

Eaton's was of inestimable value to Canadian farmers and settlers living in the remotest parts of this great dominion. Their claim was that they could and would supply the largest or the smallest requirement and guarantee satisfaction. The arrival twice yearly of the catalogue was one of the highlights of the year. In homes where there were children, such quarrels were started over who should be first to look at the new catalogue, that often pages would be torn out and scattered all over the floor before mother could rescue the coveted and much illustrated book. I believe that on the prairies a special name was coined for the catalogue. It was popularly known as the "Farmers' bible," and there is no doubt whatever that it was an extremely helpful publication for pioneer families living far from city markets and conveniences.

I would have to wait three weeks or so before I could expect to get this order of rennet from Winnipeg and start making the cheese. When Arthur brought the cheese-press with him I saw that it was a simply-made gadget, a large five-pound lard pail fitted with a tight lid to which my husband had fixed weights operated by an ingenious screw attachment which I could tighten as required. It didn't resemble our modern kitchen appliances in the least, but for making cheese it was unsurpassed. It made excellent cheese as everyone who tasted my product was quick to assure me. My husband's grandmother had brought the recipe with her to Canada in 1837 from Dorset in England and I got wonderful results with it when I used it at Dragonfly.

Soon, something new was added to my mode of existence. We began to have callers, all in the bachelor category. I hadn't even known that these lonely men were living nearby, in solitary cabins dotted along the shores of the numerous lakes of this part of the Cariboo. But apparently they knew of my existence and Randy Jackson had evidently been boasting about my cooking. In his opinion my meals rated very highly, although I found possibilities for serving fancy dishes rather limited. But I used to preserve trout in jars and when served, one could hardly tell the fish from the choicest red salmon. I browned pieces of moosemeat in a large skillet before processing it in jars in my boiler for four hours, so that it was as tender as the finest beef. Then as Randy seemed always able to get venison in season, I could usually have those tasty steaks to serve our guests.

The pattern went something like this: Randy would bring in some shyly smiling man and introduce him, "This is Hank West and he claims he isn't the least bit hungry, but I told him he would be as soon as he smelled one of your meals cooking!"

Hank West seemed to be close to seventy and resembled the pictures of Santa Claus without his red suit. With twinkling blue eyes in a ruddy and weathered face, above a thick snowy beard, he was a jolly and friendly man. He said, "Randy's right, ma'am. He sure is a lucky son-of-a-gun, fallin' into a comfortable spot like this in his old age! He says you even feed him home-made cheese?"

This called for a trip into my root cellar for a fresh cheese and after he had enjoyed a meal and gone on his way, he carried with him one of my highly-praised cheeses; how could I possibly not fall for such flattery? The recipe called for the finished product to be stored in a cool place to ripen, but the many requests I had for the cheese made that part of the process an impossibility. If there had been any such award in the Cariboo in those days as the title of Cheese Queen, I'm sure I would have cornered it.

Summertime meant a wealth of flowers and Randy taught me about herbs and their benefit to mankind. If one picked the delicate Windflower, for instance, and crushed the petals between one's fingers and sniffed at them, the scent would quickly relieve nasal congestion or head colds. There were many others that had been used successfully by the Indians for centuries.

July meant a wonderful supply of wild fruits and berries, saskatoons, a species of black raspberry, and high- and low-bush blueberries. One day I left Randy in charge of my small son and, fastening a large pail to my waist belt so as to leave both hands free to pick, took to the woods. The luscious fruits tempted me further and further afield and I lost track of time and location as I gathered the blueberries. I was absorbed in my task and reached towards a particularly tempting branch full of berries when my hand made contact with a huge furry paw and my frightened eyes stared into the too close, reddish-brown eyes of a full-grown bear.

It would have been difficult to tell which was the more startled, bruin or I. Mr. or Mrs. Bear—I never did know which it was—had its mouth stuffed with berries, leaves and twigs. Bears claw off a handful, or rather a pawful of these and cram it all into their mouths, then proceed to eliminate the twigs and leaves, eventually eating just the fruit. I noticed the dribble of waste coming from one side of bruin's mouth even though I was petrified. I was *really* scared, it was a huge bear, and I knew it was more than possible that it was a female and would likely have one or even two cubs close by. If Mamma Bear even suspected I would harm her offspring I could be in for a rough time.

At this time I recalled all the admonitions I had received about never letting animals know that you feared them. According to this advice the animals were far more likely to be afraid of me! I didn't quite feel that I could rely upon this adage. "Be nonchalant! Don't let this bear know you're scared skinny!" I told myself, bravely. "They have a sixth sense which lets them feel a human's fear, or perhaps they can *smell* fear!" All these thoughts did nothing to bolster my courage, which had flown away. Discretion seemed to be the only recourse left (with courage gone) so I cautiously withdrew my hand. The bear eyed me suspiciously as I did so. I backed away as if I were leaving the presence of royalty. Who was I to dispute the bear's territory?

Then I had another horrible thought and glanced back over my shoulder. If there were cubs, I didn't want to stumble over them, nor blunder into any more full-grown animals that might be dotted around the terrain. But apparently my escape route was clear. I glanced back at the bear and there it was, nonchalantly cramming another heap of berries into its mouth and complacently chewing although still eyeing my careful leave-taking. I left him or her to enjoy the feast and as soon as I had put some distance between it and myself, I broke into a run. By the time I reached the cabin I had spilled half the berries, but I didn't care.

I was quite out of breath as I went over to Randy sitting with the baby upon his knee talking to English Deka. When at last I could explain, I told them how scared I had been at meeting a large bear at close quarters. Randy smiled understandingly, he didn't expect a sudden transition from the tenderfoot category, but not my Indian acquaintance. Deka said disparagingly, "Brown bear, him not hurt you! Nex' time you take small can of stones and rattle 'em good. Squaws pick berries alla time that way, no scared about bears!"

At first I thought he was kidding me, and replied, "Do you mean to tell me that a bear is going to be frightened by a woman just shaking a can of stones? It sounds most unlikely to me!"

Randy smiled, "That's what all the native women use, girlie. They've been gathering berries for centuries and that's all they do. The bears don't know what it is and scare easily anyway!" I wasn't convinced, however. I tried to put myself in the bear's place. If I were a mother bruin with a cub or two alongside, it would take more than some woman rattling stones to make me back down. No! There would be no more berry-picking for me unless I had an escort, preferably carrying a gun just in case!

The berries, however, lured me back into the woods. This time I made up a picnic and fastened Roland in his carrying cradle on my back, and Randy and I made our way toward a ridge to the east of Dragonfly. He carried his rifle, hoping to see some game and get meat as well as berries. Sure enough a big buck deer had bedded down near the top of the ridge and Randy shot it, so our larder was provided for once more.

Being a city-bred woman I was still squeamish about the butchering part of game hunting. Randy told me to turn my head the other way while he gutted the carcass. He took out the heart and liver which he claimed was the best-eating part of venison, and hoisted the carcass into a jack pine. It was not very late, just after noon, and we had not picked all we wanted of the blueberries, but in this country it was good practice to bring out game as fast as possible. We returned to the cabin and Randy hunted up his saddle horses and went back to pack out the game.

By the time he returned it was dark and I had cooked the deer liver with onions for dinner. "Well, girlie! Your cooking is sure going to spoil me for going back to my bachelor existence later on! This dinner is fit for a king, and milk pudding to follow! I don't see how I *can* go back to that lonely life."

"There's no reason why you have to, Randy. When we build our big new house, why shouldn't we add another room? You could run your trapline just as well from here, couldn't you? I've been so glad to have you stay here, I feel so safe and protected. Let's keep things the way they are!" I said, and meant every word.

Randy looked at me with tears of gratitude in his eyes and to conceal his emotion he grabbed my son out of his crib and hoisted him onto his shoulder. Nothing would make him happier, he declared. He had never enjoyed life since he left his parents' home as a boy; at least, he said, not what you'd call home life. So it was all arranged and when Arthur returned for his weekend visit he found he had acquired a permanent partner.

While we had been on one of our berry-picking excursions we had come upon a wonderful stand of straight lodge-pole pine trees. People who built cabins always searched for such trees and here they were, simply ideal for our purposes and close to Dragonfly. Arthur went with Randy to inspect them and they took along a crosscut saw. At lunch time I learned that they had already cut a considerable number of trees which could be hauled to the site of our new house.

During the following week, Randy and I continued to cut the required number of poles. I fastened Roland, who was in his handy carrying cradle, to a nearby tree and I was thus free to help my friend. He planned to skin the logs out, using Molly or Daisy, and when my husband finished the season's work for Ed Martin, Randy and he planned to get the cabin built before winter set in.

By this time I was so absorbed in the daily demanding life led by pioneers that I hardly ever gave a thought to the kind of city life I had previously known. The worried letter received from my parents after they heard of our last trip over the weakening lake ice to bring back a milk cow, merely served to point up the difference between my present environment and theirs. I glanced sometimes at the theatre advertisements in the newspapers sent from Vancouver and thought, "I'd have enjoyed seeing that picture or this one," then remembered that few people nowadays had money to indulge in entertainment, anyway; the depression was drawing the entire population into a stranglehold with a monstrous grip.

The north country offered entirely different pleasures and I grew to love them. One of the chief ones was to stand at night and gaze at the beautiful and mysterious electrical display of colours which we call the Aurora Borealis. Sometimes it was a gigantic searchlight effect with glowing silver fingers probing the starlit skies. At other times, glorious canopies of vivid green or red would be poised directly overhead and were like fire-lit clouds although no earthly fires caused these vivid hues, no human hands could have devised such a diversity of lighting effects. I never grew tired of watching the glory of the Northern Lights.

I had had to bow down to defeat at the hands of mother nature in the matter of raising my own vegetables, however, and this was a sore spot with me for a long time. Anne Hodges had advised me to have my name put on Eaton's Mail Order list and when the famous spring catalogue arrived I had let everything else go while, for a few glorious hours, I enthusiastically thumbed through the pages. This finely-illustrated book permitted settlers' wives and children, and lonely trappers and miners living in remote Canadian spots and hamlets, to really live it up, in imagination at least. The women could see models gowned in lovely dresses, hats and coats, and dream of what it would be like to dress up and attend church on a bright Sunday morning. Young girls might daydream their way to romance wearing one of the lovely party dresses. Boys looked at anything or everything in the sports line from rifles to camping outfits, while their more practical fathers weighed the prices of various and much-desired pieces of farm equipment. Suffice to say, the catalogue was the stuff of many a pioneer's dream.

For my part I riveted my eyes on several pages of full-coloured pictures of garden produce and imagined that I saw row upon row of flourishing vegetables growing in my own garden. The names of each variety would be spiked to a stick at the end of each neat row for identification purposes during the period of growth when it was difficult to sort a row of beets from one of turnips. I would turn to my husband and say, "Look at these marvellous hybrid tomatoes, Arthur. Do you think this variety would grow this far north? And what kind of potato seed should we order? Roy Charlton grows some fine potatoes at Deka Lake." In my mind's eye I saw the most wonderful harvest in the fall.

So I busily filled out my lists in plenty of time for the spring planting. In due time the seeds arrived, long before the frost left the ground. I remember being terribly impatient when spring was so long delayed, accustomed as I had been to the early flowers of the mild south coast. It was late in May before I was able to plant the seeds.

Arthur and I dug and prepared the ground and finally had a sizeable patch ready for planting, and we put in our rows carefully straight so that hoeing would present no problems.

Then I sat back and waited for nature to do its part, aided and abetted by hot, constant sunshine. I was not disappointed, for in a very short time the first tiny sprouts peeked above the rich soil, rows and rows of faint green tips. We were in business! I would have scarlet runner beans on slim poles forming a fence against the encroaching woods at one end, then garden peas, broad beans, carrots, parsnips, turnips and other vegetables lined up like troops. Off to one side we planted our potato patch.

As I looked over my vegetable rows I felt as jubilant as the birds that filled the air with song. I planned upon how much of my crop I should be able to preserve for winter use. I was so sure it would be a good, large crop. That's what I thought! But eyes other than mine had already avidly sized up the growing vegetables. Perhaps I have not mentioned that rabbits here are even more prolific than elsewhere, excepting only Australia. I had seen innumerable tracks of snowshoe rabbits in winter. Often during winter excursions I had seen rabbit tracks, followed by those of some pursuing coyote or other large predator, then the spot where a few bloodied tufts of fur told the old, old story of the survival of the fittest.

However, much to the detriment of my garden, the fittest rabbits had survived, and one morning I went eagerly to inspect the growth of my carefully-tended vegetables and gave a horrified and angry shout. "For heaven's sake, Arthur, come over here! The whole garden has been ruined, just look at it!" I wailed. This was Sunday morning so my husband was at home. He joined me and offered what comfort he could, which was none at all. We stood there looking at the complete havoc wreaked by tiny sharp teeth in the night. We noticed a small movement and Arthur said, "There were more than rabbits, that's a woodchuck. I didn't know they were native to this province. The Prairies are alive with them!" He pointed to the little brown-furred animal which, not seeking publicity, darted quickly into a hole in the ground. When we investigated this we found it was an entrance to a narrow tunnel, deep in the earth, and my husband explained how the woodchuck always built both an entrance and an exit, widely spaced, so as to ensure a quick getaway when such was needed.

Jessie had warned me that I'd never be able to raise my own produce and I had proved it the hard way for myself. I then had to adjust to the fact that all our vegetables would have to come from cans. My disappointment was great, and it was very expensive to pay the high freight charges on goods hauled by the Pacific Great Eastern Railway Company. Canned fruits and vegetables do not taste as good nor contain the high amount of vitamins as fresh ones picked daily from one's own garden.

When the wild berries were ripe I made sure of having a big supply of them and my root cellar was crammed with jars of jams and preserves. I also had quite a supply of bottled trout and planned to add canned moosemeat and venison to my store of food. Arthur and Randy hoped to hunt as soon as the season opened. Only the Indians could hunt whenever they needed game; white settlers had to observe hunting seasons regulated by the Game and Fisheries Department of the government.

CHAPTER 17

Danger Comes Calling

ONE SEPTEMBER DAY Randy approached me and asked, "Will you make out your grocery order, Olive? Tomorrow I'm going to take Johnny's old wagon to Lone Butte to pick up supplies. We are expecting some of the building materials for the new cabin to arrive on today's freight shipment, and I plan to start early."

When I had milked Beauty next morning, Randy had located the team and driven away to Lone Butte. I had a full day ahead and decided to make a batch of cheese, and also planned to process some venison that Hank West had brought to me. I was frying the pieces of meat to pack into the jars for processing, when I heard horses approaching. I went outside and saw two R.C.M.P. officers dismounting. Their mounts were the finest I'd ever seen in a country that specialized in fine riding stock. The men were virile and handsome, I thought, and wouldn't have any difficulty in getting their women. Their reputation for always getting their man was well known.

The sergeant in a business-like manner jerked me back to reality with his first question as he eyed me speculatively, "Is your husband around here, ma'am?" I replied that Arthur was working at the Martin ranch on Drewry Lake and that Randy Jackson, who stayed with us, was also away. Both policemen were studying the woods behind the clearing on which the cabin was built, and scrutinizing carefully the shores of Dragonfly. The sergeant frowned and turned to me once more. "Tell me, ma'am, have you seen any strangers around your place in the past two days, I mean men who have never called at your house before?"

I said no one had been here except old Hank West and English

Deka. I asked if anything was wrong. "Well, yes, we are looking for two men, they are most likely mounted and armed." The officer looked at me appraisingly and said further, "They are wanted for murder and are from the Babine River country further north. They're very tough men and I think your husband had better come back here and stay until we find these men. We will call in at Martin's ranch and send him back. Under ordinary circumstances this is no place for a woman to be alone, but especially now!"

My heart began to pound as I looked at the sergeant. "Yes, please ask him to come home. Randy Jackson may be away overnight, he went into Lone Butte just a short time ago, so I'd appreciate it if my husband can get this message as soon as possible." I spoke quickly, and watched them mount and ride off in the direction of Martin's ranch, with growing apprehension.

I went indoors and was working again on canning the meat when I heard horses' hoofs close to the cabin once more. Could the officers be returning for some reason? But when I glanced out of the window, my heart gave a furious frightened lurch. Jumping from their saddles were two of the roughest and most savage-looking men I had ever seen. I didn't need anyone to tell me that here on my doorstep were the two wanted desperadoes hunted by the R.C.M.P. Without a doubt they had been hidden close by while the officers were questioning me; their immediate arrival after the departure of the policemen testified to that. They now felt certain that a lone woman could do nothing to prevent them from doing what they wished. I was soon to learn that I was in for trouble, if not in actual danger of being killed.

The leader of the two was a vicious-looking white man and his companion was a half-breed. They dismounted confidently and tied their sorry-looking mounts to the porch rail. Apparently they had had the cabin under surveillance for some time, perhaps since before Randy had driven away with the team. As they came towards the door I grasped the .22-calibre rifle from the gun rack, and how I wished that it were the heavy .303. But Arthur usually carried that in his saddle boot now that the hunting season was here, in the hopes of shooting some game while en route to or from Martin's place. The .22 offered little or no protection against such tough-looking antagonists, and they proved to be as brutal as their appearance.

With no hesitation, the white man took a quick step towards

145

me and pulled the gun from my hands with an evil grin. "Give me shells for this rifle! If you've got any other guns I want them, too!" he growled. He turned to the native and muttered something to him. This man went out towards the barn. These criminals were taking no chances. I guessed that if they found fresh horses on the place they would take them; their own mounts had been ridden hard and looked exhausted where they stood, heads drooping, beside the porch. I knew that it was useless to refuse and silently handed the ruffian the shells he had requested. His keen eyes detected the box that held cartridges for our .303 gun. "Where's the big rifle?" he demanded harshly. "I'll take that, too!"

I managed to jerk out the words, "My husband takes the rifle to hunt moose. It's not here now!" I was trying desperately to estimate how long it would be until I could expect help. The R.C.M.P. officers would have reached Martin's ranch quickly, I figured. But if Arthur happened to be out on the range, the message would have to be relayed on to him; I could only hope and pray that he would arrive in time.

The renegade discounted my answer and began searching for the large rifle, which he thought was hidden somewhere in the cabin. He yanked the bedding from our bed and pulled the mattress off. Then he caught sight of my baby in his crib. Roughly pulling the sleeping child from his bed, he carelessly tossed the tiny body at me. I gasped, but luckily managed to catch Roland, while the man rummaged through the blankets in the crib. The rough awakening had frightened my son and his loud, startled cries filled the room.

The half-breed returned to the cabin and whispered something to the leader. The two men started to thoroughly ransack our cabin. They took four loaves of bread, several cans of vegetables, some pound prints of butter and whatever else was edible from my cupboard shelves. They did not discover my cache of preserved meats and fish in the root cellar for the simple reason that the trap door to the cellar was hidden by a strip of carpet, but they made sure of taking whatever there was in my cupboards. Now they looked about for something in which to carry the loot and, lacking suitable sacks, these ruffians simply spread two blankets upon the floor and started to throw everything into them. We were to lose everything, even our bed coverings; my anxiety was evident to the thieves and they studied me maliciously.

This started a new fear; these men had murdered once and could suffer no more for subsequent killings should they be apprehended. Perhaps these evil glances they were now giving me meant that they had decided to do something to my son and myself! Their plans for escape and to obliterate signs of their presence here could well include disposing of the one witness to this. After I was dead and my baby with me, they could set fire to the cabin and destroy the evidence of murder in it.

These terrible thoughts were running through my mind as I crouched in a corner of the cabin with my son clutched tightly against my breast. The food was now collected and my .22 rifle thrown on top. One fellow went outside and came in with a lariat which he cut into lengths and secured the blanket bundles with them. They were muttering together now and still sending sinister glances at me. Then they discovered the pot of cooked meat on the stove, and carried it to the table with pleased grunts. They pulled pieces of meat from the pot with filthy hands and crammed them into their mouths and gulped them down half chewed, as voraciously as any starving dogs. I watched their gluttony and was thankful there was such a lot of meat in the pot; this pause to eat a meal, which undoubtedly they really needed, might delay them long enough for Arthur to yet come in time. I could do nothing but pray and try to keep hoping for aid.

The renegades were still gobbling food when the door was thrust open violently and my husband stood there with his rifle levelled, covering the intruders. He shouted, "Get your hands up! Reach!" The men, stunned, had no choice, and of course they obeyed. Without taking his eyes from them, Arthur spoke to me. "I'll need your help, dear. Put the baby down and bring those pieces of rope outside after I go out with these men. They left their rifles by the door. Take them indoors first of all, then help me truss up these fellows, they're the ones the R.C.M.P. are after!"

Arthur herded his prisoners out onto the porch and indicated one of the posts. "Tie that fellow up first, while I keep them both covered!" I looked at the half-breed fearfully, he returned a stolid gaze out of dark penetrating eyes. Dare I approach him with the rope? If he made a bid to escape and jumped me, could my husband shoot him down with me standing in the line of fire? But I decided that I hadn't much choice and, taking the rope, I went up to him as he stood with his arms still raised. I wound the rope around the

147

man's shoulders and the porch post and made a good, tight knot. "Now make another firm tie around his knees, and then fasten his hands together behind the post!" My husband gave me orders as he kept a steady eye upon both prisoners.

I did better than that, starting at the neck I wound more rope about the body of the half-breed, stopping occasionally to add an improvised knot of my own such as could never have passed scrutiny in the Boy Scouts' manual. When I was finished the native looked like a mummy swathed in rope and the effect was so comical that in spite of the tenseness of the situation, or perhaps because of it, my husband burst out laughing. "Good heavens, even Houdini couldn't get himself out of that bind!"

"If Houdini went around killing people, nobody would want him to get loose, either. At least, this man won't get free!" I retorted, and turned to help Arthur with the other prisoner.

"Here, take the rifle and keep this man covered, I'll tie him up myself," my husband said, but that proved to be an almost fatal mistake. In the split second that elapsed while the rifle was transferred to my hands, the prisoner seized the one chance for escape that he was likely to get. He dived headfirst over the porch rail and landed in a sprawling heap on the ground. Taken by surprise, Arthur yelled frantically at me, "Shoot! Shoot! Don't let that man get away!"

Without even thinking about it I swung the rifle to cover the fellow who had jumped to his feet and was gathering himself for a leap towards the nearby woods. The fact that his escape was soon to be realized, moved me to an almost involuntary action. As if hypnotized I pulled the trigger and fired. The man sprawled once more on the ground and it dawned on me that I had wounded him, perhaps even killed the man! I looked at my hands unable to believe that they could have been responsible for such a deed! The kickback from the heavy rifle caused me to stagger backwards. I was still staring at the fallen figure when my husband grasped the rifle and said, "Pull yourself together, dear! These men are murderers and wouldn't have thought twice about killing you to cover their tracks and escape the law!"

With his rifle ready he went cautiously over to examine the fallen man. Arthur straightened up and said, "It's just a leg wound, he'll live to face trial and, I suppose, cost the taxpayers a lot more money."

I couldn't feel too sorry for the taxpayers at that moment, I was so thankful that I had not killed the renegade. Still a tender heart inside, in spite of the efficient manner in which I had handled this crisis, I thought. Then Arthur called me to lend a hand with my victim. "Come and help me get him onto the porch. I will have to apply a tourniquet to stop the bleeding. If I don't he's liable to bleed to death anyway!" This matter-of-fact approach was like a cold dash of reality and I forced myself to go over and help Arthur. We each got a shoulder beneath the wounded man's arms and assisted him up the steps to the porch. He was indeed losing a lot of blood, so my husband set the gun beside the porch rail and told me to bring some strips of sheet material with which he could staunch the thigh wound. He started to cut away the buckskin pants the man was wearing.

I went inside and started to tear up a clean cotton sheet when I heard a heavy thud and a big commotion on the porch. I dashed outside and there a terrible sight met my eyes. The wounded man had somehow managed to surprise my husband and was now straddled over him. He was exerting every ounce of strength he possessed to choke Arthur to death! My husband was gasping and trying vainly to break the death-grip which the murderer had upon his throat and his face was a terrible colour. No one needed to tell me that I had to act quickly!

I grasped the heavy rifle by the barrel and jumped into the melee. Wielding the weapon like a club I brought it down on the head of the killer with all the strength I possessed. I believe at that particular moment it must have been, as in the case of Sir Galahad in Tennyson's poem, the strength of ten. The man crumpled under my savage blow and released his grip on Arthur's throat. I hurled the inert body off that of my husband, and lifted Arthur's head. Gradually the horrible colour receded from his face and he managed to gasp hoarsely, "That was too close for comfort. Thank God you kept your head, dear! I'd have been a goner in another minute!" I helped him into the cabin and onto the bed. I was shaking terribly by this time, but thankful that my nerve had held up at the crucial moment.

"Will you be all right, Arthur?" I anxiously asked my husband. "You look terrible, but I must say, not as bad as that fellow, I may really have finished him this time! But in case he comes around, I'll go out and tie him up and get the gun, it's lying right where it fell when I stunned him. But I wouldn't trust that man even in that condition!"

With no namby-pamby pretense of handling the still-unconscious man with care, I grasped his arms and trussed him firmly to the porch post in the same manner that his companion was fastened. I wanted no further harrowing attacks from either of these renegades; I finally realized it was their lives or ours! I looked at the prisoner, propped in a sitting position against the post, and saw that his leg wound was still bleeding. Something would have to be done to stop it. I went inside and told Arthur what I had done and he felt that we could attempt first aid together. "But he'll have to remain tied, I'm afraid to trust him," I asserted as I gathered bandages again.

Then I heard a team approaching the cabin, followed by an amazed shout from Randy. "Whoa there! What in the world's been going on here?" Our friend rushed inside with an agility surprising for his sixty-seven years. "Looks like a scene from one of those westerns! Blood and all! Those two fellows are the ones the R.C.M.P. men want?" he queried. Then he looked at Arthur more closely. "Say, just what did happen? When I got into town the news was everywhere about these men that the R.C.M.P. were chasing. I got a few things together and drove right back. Didn't figure this young lady should be alone here with murderers in the vicinity!"

"It's been a sort of graduation day for greenhorns around here today. We both got in on the act, but the bloodiest of the two men is my wife's trophy. If she hadn't kept her head and been able to act quickly, I'd have been a goner, myself!" Arthur related proudly.

I disclaimed all the credit. "Indeed, Randy, if Arthur had not arrived when he did, those desperadoes would likely have finished both Roland and me. The story would have ended much differently I fear."

Arthur and Randy took the bandages, which I had started to prepare before all the excitement started, and went out to inspect our victim. I set about restoring the room to some kind of order. I placed all the food back in the cupboards and the blankets back on the bed. I looked at our son who had gone back to sleep in the crib where I had hurriedly set him down while I went to assist his father with the capture of the criminals. I gave silent thanks for our safety.

Randy came in for hot water. "Will you fix me a quick meal,

girlie? We're going to make that fellow as comfortable as possible, but naturally we'll leave them tied up. Arthur says you insist upon that and I don't blame you. They are tough hombres! Then I'll ride up towards Canim Lake, the officers told Arthur and Ed Martin that they would continue their hunt in that locality. The sooner we contact the officers the sooner we'll get rid of our prisoners, eh?"

Our friend rode away and I prepared a meal for ourselves. The renegades had eaten all the meat brought by old Hank West, but that fact had made all the difference in the day's happenings. When my husband remarked that he supposed we should feed our prisoners, I replied somewhat edgily, "They shouldn't need another ounce of food, they ate a whole pot of venison before you came to the rescue. Somehow I don't feel the least bit sorry for those men!"

I just didn't relish the idea of having those murderers attached to the supports of our porch even for one night, but we had no choice. My husband slept the sleep of the just, but all night long I imagined I heard suspect sounds on the porch and I kept popping in and out of bed. I kept up this watchdog act all the dragging hours of darkness; the prisoners, also wide awake, would turn their eyes keenly upon me whenever I went near them. But somehow the night ended and I eagerly looked forward to the arrival of the R.C.M.P. officers and Randy Jackson later in the day.

In mid-afternoon the R.C.M.P. men arrived and confirmed our belief that these were the wanted criminals. "Congratulations! It took courage to tackle these fellows," the sergeant told us, then smiling to me, "The 'Mounties' aren't the only ones to get their man. You didn't do so badly in that department yourself, ma'am."

I served the officers an early supper and, carefully guarded by the policemen, the prisoners were untied and provided with a meal before leaving Dragonfly. Then the officers arranged a sling between two of the horses in which to transport the wounded prisoner. The other was mounted and his hands securely fastened. "By the way," the sergeant said as he bade us farewell, "there's a reward posted for the capture of these men. I think the amount is two thousand dollars. You will be notified by the commissioner's office and they will be mailing you a cheque."

"A cheque for two thousand dollars! You must be kidding?" I gasped incredulously. "Why, that's a fortune!" and I looked at the prisoners almost kindly as they all rode away.

Suddenly the tension of the past thirty-six hours snapped.

More real danger had been crowded into them than my husband and I had ever experienced before. Even the happy ending seemed somehow unreal. Randy and Arthur did a sort of celebration dance in front of the cabin. "Whoopee! Two thousand dollars! I can't believe it," shouted my husband gleefully. Then they pulled me into the circle and Randy said, "Well, we'll have some cattle paid for before we even build a corral and barn to hold them." I think we all spent that reward money in two thousand separate ways in the time that elapsed before it actually was received in the mail. What a grand and glorious opportunity for us all!

CHAPTER 18

Roping a Bull Moose

SEPTEMBER CAME, BRISK AND BRIGHT. One day, while Randy was building a corral, and Arthur was working at the round-up for the fall cattle sales at Ed Martin's ranch, I was doing a few chores about the cabin when I saw old Hank West ride into the clearing. He was leading the most beautiful little filly I had ever seen, her hide an unusual golden tan and with a striking blonde mane and tail. Hank got spryly down from his saddle and said to me, "Well, young lady, how do you like your new saddle pony, hmm?"

"I don't have a saddle pony, yet, Hank," I told him, "but now that we're going to be in the money, I'll be able to get one."

"Oh yes, you do have a horse. This little filly is for you. I caught her, gentled her especially for you. She's so tame now, I declare she'd eat out of your hand, 'specially if there's some carrots handy," laughed the old man genially.

"D'you mean that you found this filly in a band of wild horses and caught her and broke her to the saddle yourself, Hank?"

"Yep, I was trailin' a bunch of them cayuses over to Buffalo Creek and I figured this pretty little creature could be gentled so even a little tenderfoot woman I knew could ride her!" Hank West then told me how it was he earned his living. I had always thought he ran a trapline like Randy.

"I make my livin' by riding out into the hills until I meet up with a band of wild horses, there's plenty of bands in the Cariboo. Then I cut out the best and most likely-lookin' ones, rope 'em and drive 'em to my corrals. Then I break 'em to the saddle, gentle 'em and sell 'em to the owners of these new dude ranches that's springin' up all over the range country!"

I believe that Hank had passed the seventy-year mark, but his marvellous physique belied the fact, his agility could deceive anyone into thinking he was a much younger man. Still it was very difficult for me to picture him riding boldly into a band of wild horses which were led and protected by a rambunctious stallion. It certainly was dangerous work, cutting out certain members of a band of such freedom-loving creatures and stealing them from the king-pin of the band. It didn't seem to faze this wonderful old man. I looked at him admiringly and said, "It was very kind of you to think about me, Hank, and I most certainly appreciate it. But I can afford to buy the filly from you now. We had a stroke of good luck last week, we're going to be rich!"

Randy had approached and heard my last words. "Good luck she calls it. Plenty of pluck is more like it! Hank, did you know that this little girl and her husband captured those two fellows wanted for murder that the R.C.M.P. were hunting for around these parts?"

The veteran of the hills looked at me wonderingly, then burst out fervently, "No kiddin', young lady, you can't call yourself a tenderfoot any more. And I always thought that city folk was sissies, too!"

I laughed and stood admiring the filly. "When we get this reward money I'm going to buy a lot of things I've just been dreaming of until now. This pretty filly will be the first, I'm going to name her Blondie. Thank you so much for bringing her, Hank." I went indoors and prepared a lunch for the men. When it was ready I called Randy and Hank to the table and as usual they were effusive in their praise of whatever I set before them. I never could get over how appreciative these wilderness bachelors were of home-cooked meals.

"Did you say this was moosemeat, ma'am?" enquired Hank. "It tastes exactly like prime beef, don't it now, Randy?" It was true that after I had browned moosemeat in a skillet and then put the pieces in preserving jars and processed them for four hours in boiling water, the gamey taste of moose disappeared and one could scarcely tell the difference between it and beef.

Hank West looked thoughtful and then came up with an idea. "I'll tell you what, little girl. How would you like to bottle some moose and deermeat for me? A winter's supply let's say, in payment for that filly, since you're so set on payin' me for her?"

"Why certainly, Hank. I'd be glad to preserve some game for

154

you. I'll make a start on it just as soon as Arthur or Randy can shoot a moose or deer," I assured the old fellow.

"Don't worry your head none where the meat's comin' from. I'll go out tomorrow and hunt and I'll bring over pieces of meat the right size for you to handle without too much trouble," said the old-timer, who was apparently as fine a hunter as he was at his job of catching and taming wild horses.

"Just like that, eh?" Randy remarked. "You'll go out and get a moose tomorrow! I've been hunting for signs of moose for some time and haven't had any luck. The one time I could have got a buck deer my rifle was on the fritz. There's something the matter with the firing pin, so I lost out on the deer, too."

"Well, now's the time to get your moose, Randy. Try over towards Buffalo Creek, I usually have good luck there. Come the end of October the bulls will be givin' up their bachelor freedom and hidin' themselves in the dark muskeg or in some deadfall country where you'll have the devil's own job findin' a bull. This is the time to bag your moose, and they're good eatin'! They've had all summer to browse and eat their fill of good grass and nothin' to bother 'em at all." The old woodsman spoke with authority.

"What do you mean, Hank, about the moose hiding somewhere? My husband is hoping to hunt moose as soon as he is through at Martin's ranch, after the round-up. We thought moose would be in good supply until late November and we'd have plenty of time," I interrupted.

"Of course, you young people are newcomers to the country, so I'd better tell you somethin' about moose," replied the old-timer. "It's this way. The cows have their calves to take care of all summer and they don't want the bulls around. So in late May or early June the females kick the bulls out of the herds. The bulls form a sort of bachelor club, four or five together, roam around to the best grazing spots. They can lie in the lake shallows when the flies get bothersome, just livin' the life of Riley, you might say. If you shoot one then, the meat is in prime condition, but once the bulls hole up alone and go on a starvation diet for a couple of weeks, hunters know that the bull moose is toughenin' himself up for the ruttin' season.

"At the end of these two weeks you wouldn't know it was the same moose. He's ornery, empty-bellied and ready to fight anything. He scrapes his hoofs on rocks until he's got a knife edge on 'em. He butts his horns against trees and tries his strength in every way he can think of until he feels rough enough and tough enough to take on anything that moves. Then he comes stormin' out of the deadfalls looking for the herds of cows. *Then* is the time you've got to watch out for Mister Moose! Worst of all is a rogue moose because he's been run out of the herd by the younger and stronger bulls. This means he's on his own and is not allowed the privileges he used to enjoy with the cows when he was leader of the herd. He becomes very savage and anyone meetin' him, even though armed, is up against a tough situation. Rogue bulls have been known to charge at horses and their riders and unless a man is really alert and ready with his rifle he could be killed!"

"Just think! All this time I've been scared of meeting with a grizzly, when rogue moose seem like a greater threat!" I called out to Hank as he rode away into the trail. What a lot I had to learn about the north woods and the wild creatures living in them.

The old woodsman was back next afternoon to back up his promise of bringing the moosemeat. He had two saddlebags filled with pieces which were ready to cook and process in bottles. "This will keep you busy for a while and I'll bring more. There are some fresh steaks which would do fine for supper tonight, though," he hinted in his genial fashion. I took the hint and started to cook the succulent steaks. We were just sitting down at the table when we heard a horse coming through the trail. It was my husband who had stopped in on his return from helping with Ed Martin's cattle drive out to the railroad corrals. He informed us that his work was finished there for the season.

"I'm just in time for a steak dinner, I see," he said, "and here's something we've all been looking forward to!" He held out an official-looking envelope which, sure enough, contained the reward cheque. "Randy and I are going to be looking for good beef cattle. In fact Ed had promised to sell me a few of that prize herd he bought from John Winters before he left the Cariboo." Crowded around the little table though we were, that was, I dare say, the most festive meal that had ever been served in the cabin.

While I washed up later, the men sat comfortably talking. Arthur gave us the latest gossip from town; in Lone Butte they were still discussing the capture of the desperadoes by the new young people on Dragonfly Lake, he said. Our own stock had risen appreciably and we were definitely out of the greenhorn category.

Arthur planned to go and find the team in the morning, since after Randy had finished hauling the logs for building he had turned them out to pasture. Hank bedded down in the barn with Randy that night so that he could start early to go to town in the morning for supplies. Randy planned a day's hunting in the Buffalo Creek meadows where Hank had advised him to look for moose.

"If you won't be needing your rifle tomorrow, Arthur, may I borrow it? I've been having trouble with the firing pin on my gun and lost a big buck deer last week because my rifle was acting up, and I'm still mad about it," Randy told my husband.

"Sure, you take it, Randy," Arthur said, "Jessie has been asking me when Olive could get up for a visit. I'll take her with me tomorrow if I can borrow one of your saddle ponies." He had not yet seen my new pony, having been at Martin's place when Hank had brought her to me.

The same evening that Blondie had arrived, Randy had come from the barn carrying something wrapped carefully in a blanket. He uncovered a brand new saddle which he said Johnny Winters had bought for his bride-to-be when she was expected to marry him and make her home in the Cariboo. Randy remembered how disappointed Johnny was when his fiancée did not like this lonely country and made it necessary for him to sell his prize herd of cattle and follow her back to Texas. Randy thought Johnny must have forgotten all about the saddle when selling his possessions, because it was still hanging in Winters' barn.

Next morning Randy put the new saddle upon Blondie and I ventured up on her back. Just broken to the saddle though she was, the pony was everything Hank had promised she would be. I had expected a little skittishness, but no, you'd have thought she knew, with the uncanny wisdom sometimes called horse sense, that her new owner was also an inexperienced rider and she behaved in the most decorous manner when I took my first ride on her. I was very happy and said to Randy, "When we get that reward money I'll mail Johnny the price of his saddle. From what you tell me, he isn't likely to ever come back here to run his ranch or need this saddle for his wife. It's such a nice one!"

When Arthur went to the barn next morning to saddle Speed, he was surprised to see a strange pony in the corral. Already Blondie and Speed appeared to have become attached to each other. He was leading both horses when he returned. "I declare!

The things that happen while I'm away from home! Randy tells me that you're going to earn this pony by canning moosemeat for Hank West. I've got a smart wife and some very good friends, that's certain."

He took Roland up in front of him on his saddle because I felt the little one would be safer there, not that I doubted Blondie's behaviour but I was an inexperienced rider, nonetheless, and wanted to get a feeling of more confidence before I took my son on my saddle. When we arrived at Martin's house, Jessie came eagerly out to greet us and exclaimed when she saw my pony, "What a little beauty, and her golden mane! I wish I had hair such a lovely blonde colour. By the way, I'm glad you could come, my hair needs a touch-up job done on it."

Arthur rode off to hunt our team which had been seen in this vicinity while the round-up was in progress. Ed went about his work in the corrals, so we had the house to ourselves. I looked at my friend's head. "Yes, the tell-tale grey is beginning to show at the roots again, so we'll get at that job first of all." Jessie was as garrulous as ever and wanted first-hand details of the adventures Arthur and I had recently experienced. I had to tell the story all over again and said that the reward money had just been received, and what we planned to do with it.

"How're you ever goin' to settle down to bein' an ordinary rancher's wife after all these exciting things that have been happenin' to you since you came to the Cariboo? You're apt to be bored!" Jessie exclaimed exuberantly. "You should write a book."

"Maybe I will if I ever get time to write about it," I replied, "but I think right now that I wouldn't mind being a little bored. Peace and quiet would be quite welcome."

We had finished lunch when we heard a rapid drumming of horse's hoofs and Arthur dashed into the clearing and was yelling excitedly as Ed went outside. "Hey, Ed, lend me a rifle, will you? I've got a bull moose roped and tied back there beside the old wagon road to Buffalo Creek!"

"You've got a *what* roped and tied? You didn't say bull moose, did you, lad?" replied Ed with a grin of disbelief spreading over his rugged features.

"That's what I said, Ed. Lend me your gun, will you? That moose was mad enough to yank out the tree he was tied to and take to the tall timbers!" yelled my husband, his usual calm gone with the wind.

"Oh, come off it, man. Quit trying to kid the troops! You don't expect me to believe a green cowhand could rope and tie a bull moose, do you?" Ed laughed derisively. "*That,* I've got to see!"

Arthur exploded, his patience gone. "Well then, don't bother trying to believe me, just lend me a rifle so I might get there in time to shoot the animal. The one time I really needed my gun I didn't have it with me!" This finally convinced Ed Martin and he sprinted for his horse in the corral near the barn, calling out to Jessie as he went, to hand Arthur his rifle on the gun rack.

"My goodness, this doesn't happen every day, I'd like to go and see, too!" I exclaimed, almost as excited as my husband was. "Ed, bring my horse, too, I want to ride along with you men." Then I was galloping after them, due west to an overgrown wagon road. Soon we could hear a loud drumming series of thuds and arrived at the scene where, looking almost larger than life-size, was a huge moose. He was still fastened securely to the tree with the only lariat which could have withstood such a strain as the beast was putting upon it as he struggled to free himself. This was an immensely strong lariat made of woven rawhide and it bound the terrified moose against the jack pine. My husband put an end to the captured animal's agony with one shot, and although the moose sagged in its bonds, Arthur fired a second shell to make doubly certain.

I had never seen a moose before and was amazed at its size. "I'll be darned, Arthur! You really did rope a bull moose—and got away with it!" said Ed admiringly. "Real beginner's luck I call it. He's a big one, should dress out over nine hundred pounds. I'll ride back and bring the team and wagon to haul in the meat. You can handle the butchering part of it, I guess?"

I rode back to his ranch with him because my city blood always showed itself when this gory task had to be performed. I had been accustomed to seeing meat displayed on trays in the butcher shops in town and since coming to the wilderness when I had been given huge chunks of game, still dripping blood, to cook and serve, I suffered some queasy feeling in my stomach.

When I rejoined Jessie, who had taken charge of my son, I told her, "I still don't know how Arthur did rope that great animal. After all the things we've been hearing about moose, especially at this time of year, I'd have been scared stiff. But now we have some game and Arthur had been so anxious to get a moose. How are you fixed for game, Jessie? I'd think there'd be sufficient to feed any number of people."

Some time later the men returned, bringing the butchered game. At the dinner table Jessie demanded to hear all the details. "I don't know how it happens, but you young people seem to have all the excitement these days. Ed has lived in the bush all of his life and nothing ever happens to him. Tell us how you roped the moose."

"It's probably a case of fools rushing in; if I had Ed's years of experience behind me, I would probably have used discretion no doubt, too. Anyway, I was moseying along that old wagon road keeping my eyes peeled for signs of horses because there is good grazing all through that part, when I suddenly saw moose signs. Speed saw the moose first, his ears shot forward and I followed his gaze and saw this big creature standing still beside the trail, staring at us.

"He was considering us and whether to stand or run. Finally he gave himself the benefit of the doubt. Without really having any plan of action I urged my horse a few yards closer to the moose, but Speed, having a trifle more than his share of horse sense, was chary about this job. He cocked one ear forward, one back, and half turned his head to look at me, not quite believing that I knew what I was doing. Being a top horse and having more than proved it during the round-up here at Ed's ranch, Speed did know a thing or two, so he balked at going too close to such an adversary. Those big horns were no joke and he edged forward, gingerly.

"The moose lowered his heavy head, hunched up his powerful shoulders and glared menacingly. Though the horse snorted with fear, I stood in my stirrups and swung my lariat, one end of which was fastened to the saddlehorn. As the rope whirled out and over him the moose turned and dashed for the trees, just a split second too late, however, for the rawhide slipped down about his horns. The next instant the rope tightened about his head as Speed, who was trained to the job and knew what was expected of him, turned quickly and showed his tail to the moose. The lariat drew taut, the captive moose was jerked abruptly to a standstill. All this happened in about a half minute and there we were in a sort of a quandary because the horse had never had to handle such a weight as he now found at the end of the rope.

"I had the idea that if my horse and I could haul the moose into the woods and I could rope him to a tree, I would have the situation under control. But the animal did not budge an inch, he was rooted to the spot as if he had grown there. Then I had a new worry, I felt my saddle slip a trifle and feared that the cinch might loosen. It occurred to me right then that I had bitten off more than I could chew, as the saying goes. I felt about for my small jack-knife with the idea of cutting the lariat and releasing the moose. There was too much tension on the rope to allow me to unfasten my end of the lariat, so cutting it was the only answer.

"Just as I was about to cut him loose, the enraged animal jerked viciously back on the rope. Speed lurched sideways and back upon his haunches and the knife spun out of my hand to the ground. I figured I'd done enough fool tricks and taken enough chances without trying to jump down and grab the knife from under my horse's plunging hoofs, and things looked bad for us at that moment. It was the moose's natural instinct to take cover that was the deciding factor. He pounded the ground with his flashing hoofs while turf flew in all directions and then charged in our direction which was also the way the timber lay.

"Well, Speed needed no urging, he had to keep out of the way of that cyclone of hoofs which was only the length of the rope behind us. Then a lucky coincidence saved us. Just before we hit the timber a large jack pine loomed in our path and it happened that Speed chose one side while the moose dashed past the tree on the opposite side. There we were, see-sawing with the rope around the trunk of the jack pine, terrified moose on one end, frightened horse on the other! Speed was practically out of hand by now, but I had to do something! I coaxed him, plunging and snorting as he was, to step around another tree close to the first one. Then again around this tree, pulling the furious game animal close to the original jack pine trunk. A few more cautious turns gave me enough play in the rope to be able to unfasten it from the saddle-horn. I put a couple of half-hitches in my end to secure the twists made in it around the second tree. I felt satisfied that Mister Moose was fairly well trussed for a while at least and raced back here for a gun. You know the rest."

I had sat there, white-faced, listening to my daring young husband tell this tale, thinking how close to death he had been! But Ed spoke his piece, "Darn it all, Arthur, didn't you realize that that moose could have charged you and killed both you and the horse. We could easily have had a widow and an orphan on our hands!"

"Yes, indeed, I did realize it, but a little too late; by that time, I was too busy figuring a way out to do any other thinking. I owe my life to Speed the way I see it; there's a horse in a million!" said Arthur. In this modest fashion my husband gave his mount most of the credit for his safety and the successful termination of the roping incident.

Later, I heard of one or two such ropings, usually by experienced cowhands, but it was generally regarded as not run-of-the-mill procedure in moose hunting.

CHAPTER 19

Our Cabin

NEXT MORNING ED MARTIN, accompanied by Jessie, took time off from their busy work schedule to drive to Dragonfly with the team and wagon, hauling our cut-up sections of meat. We had no ice storage at present and this meant that ahead of me stretched days and days of processing the moose in order to preserve it. I could see that I would have no idle moments for some time to come.

Hank West had not yet departed on his trip to Lone Butte, so I put as much of the game as his saddlebags would hold and sent it to Anne Hodges. Ralph was not permitted to hunt and she had far too many chores about the ranch to perform to allow time for getting any game, but they were accustomed to doing favours for so many of the bachelors in the district, that these men gladly supplied Anne with all the game meat she wanted.

We walked over to our new home-site with our guests and Ed commented on our choice of location. "You're wise to get down from that ridge where Johnny built his cabin. He realized too late what a task he would always have, carrying water from the lake up that steep bank."

"Yes, that was the first thing we realized. I was an engineer while working in the city and I knew that if we were to build at this lower level that we should have enough of a fall from that creek that I could pipe it into the house and have running water. We've got visions of indoor plumbing for the future. When we dream, we dream big, but plumbing is a practical possibility with that stream so handy," Arthur told them as they looked at the huge collection of long, straight logs, peeled and waiting to be turned into a log home.

Suddenly my spouse noticed a big mound of large stones, piled near the logs. This represented hours of tiring labour on my part all during the past summer, while Arthur was away. He inquired of me, somewhat facetiously, "Are you planning one of those steam-bath huts like the Indians use, my dear?"

"Funny, funny!" I told him. "These stones, Arthur, are for you to use in building me a fireplace for the living room of our new home. I've heard you and Randy complaining about those blocks of fuel wood so full of knots that even Paul Bunyan would find it impossible to split with an axe. This will solve that knotty problem and provide a homelike atmosphere to our new house. There's nothing cosier than a roaring fire to keep winter at bay in the north country."

"But I'm not at all sure I can make a fireplace that won't smoke us out-of-doors!" Arthur said doubtfully. I thought he was under-estimating his ability, and I told him that if building a large log cabin didn't faze him, there was no reason why a fireplace should. I produced a rudimentary drawing of what I hoped our house would look like when completed and Jessie and Ed concluded that when it came to dreaming, I was way ahead of everybody. The picture showed a neat stone chimney going up one wall of the future living room. But I held my ground against their derision. After all, every building that had ever been made on earth had had its conception in someone's brain first.

While we were eating lunch I was dismayed to see a fine rain of dust descending from the shake roof and falling down upon the dishes of food on the table. This had never happened before, it had to wait until I was entertaining guests! Jessie laughed and said, "Think nothing of it! You should have been with us last Christmas; we were at dinner at Jack Purcell's house and the whole darned roof caved in on top of the turkey and fixin's! What a mess! Mary Purcell was so peeved and the dinner was ruined, to say nothin' of the roof! Seems it was a pretty old roof and the sods on top of the poles had moved under so much snow and when things dried out, the earth just pushed through those old shakes! Glory be!" My friend's laughter was contagious and we all joined in the merriment, but I became very thoughtful and after our friends had gone home I told Randy and Arthur that we ought to have a conference on log-cabin structure.

"You mean about this fireplace idea of yours?" my husband asked. "Well, we'll have a try at it and see what we can do."

I looked at him and replied, "Thank you, Arthur, but it's something more pressing—roofing and flooring. I think now we have this money which we hadn't counted upon, we can afford to put a real ceiling of lumber beneath the shakes and also have a smooth board floor. That's important because soon our son will be crawling and learning to walk. Let's see to it that he can do this without accumulating countless slivers. I would like some guarantee that *our* roof won't collapse about our ears later, too!"

The men looked at each other in dismay. "We had really earmarked almost all of the money to buy really good Hereford stock. There won't be much left over to buy lumber, but the roof we're proposing to build here will be as durable as any shingled roof. Shakes don't require rocks and sod on top to anchor them to the roof poles. So nothing will go wrong with that type of roofing," Arthur replied.

I was dismayed, too, but also determined and stood up for my rights. "I'm sorry, boys, but half of that reward money is mine, and I'm all for more creature comforts in the house and fewer creatures in the barn. So I've decided to spend some of my share to buy some finished lumber for floors, ceilings, and if possible to line the walls of the rooms. Let's figure out what we shall require from that mill at Alexis Creek."

The men gave in with good grace and we made out our list of building materials. They rode off together next day and finally located Molly and Daisy near Drewry Lake. The following day they made the trip to town and to the lumber mill further away. I spent each day processing the large amount of moosemeat on hand. This had to be finished because I planned to help wherever possible with the actual building of the new log home. There was a large amount of sphagnum moss still to be collected and hauled in from the forests, and this I would have to push into the cracks between the logs and in the notched ends as the men raised each alternate row of logs into the correct place.

Randy had come up with a money-saving idea, too. Some of the straight logs he had cut and hauled could be sawn into boards at the mill, and they had chosen a number for this purpose and took them to the mill at Alexis Creek. These made quite satisfactory floor boards which my husband said he would plane to a better smoothness when they were laid. The mill was a small one, not too well equipped to produce finely finished lumber for which

Arthur was told they had few requests. We were being very ritzy, it seemed.

There was another time-consuming task which had to be done before the actual erection of the house could be started. The men put large hay racks on the wagon and went every day for two weeks to gather wild hay from the meadows in the district. With a number of cows and the horses to feed through a long winter, they needed a large quantity of hay. Later they planned to clear several acres in the same way that Ed Martin had done and plant them with feed crops, which were what was needed to produce good beef herds. But for this first year on our pre-empted land, the wild hay must be hauled and used as winter feed.

Randy had foresightedly cut enough logs for a large barn too, and the men proposed to build the barn quickly so that most of the hay could be pitched into the loft away from weather spoilage. Speed, although somewhat disdainful of the down-grading, was pressed into service while the team hauled loads of hay. With a single harness and a small stoneboat, I went into the woods and gathered tons of moss, at least it seemed like tons, and Speed dragged the loads to the building site. We were now just about ready to start the building of the cabin and anxious to get at it before the first snows heralded the long northern winter. Our plan called for the cabin to be ready for occupancy before the cold weather came.

The building site had been levelled and at last Arthur and Randy started to put down the first four logs that were to form the sills. The forty-foot length ran east and west, so that the living room and kitchen would face onto Dragonfly, the main door was in that wall also. The thirty-foot logs were laid north to south. To be certain that the foundation logs were absolutely level, lacking modern tools and aids, my husband used an old-fashioned method. A bottle of water was fastened onto the middle of each log. When the log was lying exactly level, a small bubble appeared on the surface of the water. Then a cord was attached to the bottle and stretched to the end of the log, which was raised or lowered as necessary to ensure a perfect level.

Sometimes the notch into which each end of a log was snugly fitted, would need a trifle more cutting. Before these final cuts were made and the log dropped into place, I packed the fibrous moss into the bottom of the notched portion. Then I went the length of the logs forcing moss into the cracks and plastering

166

them with mud. When the walls were a depth of four logs, poles were placed at a slight slope against the logs and, by means of other poles used as levers, the men were able to raise the succeeding logs with a minimum of effort. This rudimentary knowledge of engineering saved us a great deal of back-breaking labour.

I had insisted that we have plenty of windows. I had visited a couple of bachelor cabins in the district and found they boasted one tiny window only, and it was almost as dark as night indoors and very gloom-making in my opinion. So we were going to have plenty of light in the new home, even though it was very difficult to haul windows from town over rough trails in a wagon. If we could wait until winter when sleighs were smoother travelling it would be easier, but we planned to occupy the house before winter arrived.

Then Hank returned from his shopping trip and produced a broadaxe from his saddlebag. These commodities are as rare as the Dodo in civilized parts of the world, but many could be located in the Cariboo and Hank said he had borrowed this one. After dinner he set out to prove he was well advanced in the use of a broadaxe by starting to smooth the insides of the logs already laid. Next day he offered his services with the building and as each log was placed he jumped up on it and got busy with that broadaxe. Again I was obliged to marvel at this elderly man's endurance and ability to do a hard day's work.

My task was to stuff moss and mud into every crack and cranny. Randy came along to inspect my work. He then asked me to watch him and learn how to add the finishing touch to a well-built log house. "To complete this part, these thin poles that I have stacked over there, have to be fastened along the intervening cracks between each layer of logs. D'you think you're able to do that? It makes a perfect insulation because these poles prevent the moss from falling out later."

I assured him that I could do this work, leaving him free for the heavier jobs. They had nearly reached roof level now and I was excited to see what fast progress was being made. At dinner that night the men were discussing something which appeared to be posing problems. This bugbear was referred to each time as "she" and I grew more and more intrigued as Randy said, "It's going to be the dickens of a job getting her up there, she might get loose on us and roll right down the other side!"

Arthur replied, "Her weight is what's bothering me, but I've

figured how to support her once we get up to the peak. We'll need good, strong stringers put down at the roof level and from these we can have pole supports to take the weight and stop any sagging." The reason that men always designate any trouble-making things such as storms, droughts and labour that is difficult to do, as female, remains a mystery to me; thus, our ridgepole was a "she" and the men were prepared to deal with her accordingly. I rather dreaded the raising of Madame Ridgepole.

The roof stringers were laid and, at intervals of ten feet, strong pole supports erected, notched securely into the stringers. With three strong men dominating the scene, My Lady Ridgepole was not at all ornery as they had predicted she might be. With ropes around her and sinewy hands hauling, she knew better than to resist. Much sooner than they hoped, she had been hauled to the peak and set firmly on the gable ends and on those properly-spaced supporting stringers. This *really* was an occasion for celebration. I left the scene and went to broil venison steaks.

Hank had foresightedly brought some of that potent potato whiskey from town, so the men rewarded their labours with what they called a couple of snorts. I, from my own experience at New Year's, decided to give the stuff a wide berth. It was now fairly smooth going. The rafters, constructed of light poles, went on quickly and then Randy and Hank started putting the large shakes on for the roof. Randy had been fortunate in finding the right kind of spruce trees for making shakes. He needed trees on which the branches did not grow too close to the ground, because branches mean knots and the latter make poor shakes. Randy had made perfect shakes for the job.

Arthur, meanwhile, produced two sturdy doors from some of the planed boards. Though not the finished product of a lumber mill, his doors were not clumsy and a great deal less expensive. He made sashes for doors and windows. The latter had to be bought from glass manufacturers in Vancouver and brought up by P.G.E. freight, a costly operation, but necessary in this case. Arthur warned me as he fitted the sashes in place between the log walls of the cabin, "When these windows are installed, you'd better treat them as if they're made of gold, because it sure cost plenty to get them into this neck of the woods!"

The ceiling boards were put up and enough of these had been planed to make inside wall coverings over the logs. Our living room was, so Hank said, big enough for a schoolroom. It measured twenty-five feet and the kitchen a handy fifteen feet long. When one considers how many uses a Cariboo kitchen was put to, lots of room was, in my opinion, a positive necessity. The cramped quarters of Winters' cabin had been slowly but surely giving me a phobia of some kind. I was secretly gloating upon my future living quarters. Two spaces for doors out of the living room were cut and one led into the room which was to be Randy's. The other door led into a tiny hallway from which one would go into two more bedrooms, ours and a little room for our son, and wonder of wonders a washroom with, we hoped, running water, a lavatory and later even a bathtub!

We planned to make all our furniture during the winter months. Bunk beds were very popular in this part of the country, and Randy said he would put his up; we had our bed and mattress to put into our own room and the baby's crib into the small one. I had written to my parents telling them of our adventures with the outlaws and Arthur's feat of roping the bull moose. I think this information rather floored them temporarily, but when they had rallied around and my mother remembered the reward, she went off to the first furniture sale she saw advertised in the Vancouver newspapers and her next letter informed me that "for a song" she had bought a comfortable couch and two chesterfield chairs and a small dining room set which I could send her the money for later. I told Arthur and all he could say was, "Heavens, whatever next? I suppose we have to go to town with the wagon again and haul this stuff out now?"

We planned a gala house-warming party and naturally I needed these articles of furniture, so Arthur drove out and hauled in this load and I was very pleased with my mother's astute buying spree. She really had obtained the things at a bargain price and I sat down and thanked her and enclosed the cost of the furniture in a letter right away. When the rooms had been floored and my new possessions arranged, I felt like a queen, but much happier, I've no doubt. My spouse had to admit that our home was just about perfect, even if it meant a couple of cows fewer in the barn.

While Arthur was hauling the furniture from town, Randy had tentatively made a start on the rock chimney. Now all three men busied themselves with it and, much sooner than they had hoped, they had what I declared was an architect's dream of a stone fireplace at one end of the large living room. With that done my home was habitable and Kitchen Queen was hauled from the little cabin where she had always seemed a bit high and mighty, and installed in the new roomy kitchen. The rest of our crowded belongings were moved into the new house and more of the potato whiskey was obtained for the house-warming which we planned upon completing the building of Spencers' log cabin.

As we expected, news of our house-warming reached many ears and soon the new home was filled to overflowing. The builders received a much deserved ovation from the male visitors, while my living room with modern furniture filled less fortunate women with envy. One could almost wish that more renegades might choose our wilderness as an escape route so that other alert homesteaders might capture them and collect rewards. But outlaws don't lurk behind every tree and such good fortune as was ours does not come to everyone.

We were comfortably established when the first snows started drifting through the "Isch-ka-bibble" and Randy began to get his traps ready. For him winter was the busiest season. Our home was cozy against the first cold blasts of Arctic weather, our corrals held a reassuring number of cattle and the future looked rosy. We had no regrets at all about leaving the city and becoming pioneers in the Cariboo.

PHOTOS FROM THE AUTHOR'S COLLECTION

Courtesy of Paul Spencer.

Captions adapted from handwritten notations on the back of the photos.

Art, baby Roland and the team, Dan and Molly.

The land, across the lake, that I hope will be ours. It borders Dragonfly Lake on one side, and Hathaway Lake, just over the first ridge, on the other.

Olive riding Dan. Her first time on a horse.

Three generations: Grandfather Jim, father Art, and son Roland.

Art with his twenty pound trout.

The neighbours, going to town.

Olive and son Roland, the day the ice went out on Dragonfly Lake.

Art with the team, at –40° F.

ABOUT THE AUTHOR

OLIVE SPENCER LOGGINS shared
many adventures and much happiness
with her husband, Arthur, during their
forty years of marriage. After his death
in 1965, she travelled in Ontario visiting
their two sons and other relatives.

In 1970 she met and married
Clinton Loggins, a Texan with a fine
hand for gardening. They had six years
together before his death. Olive
Spencer Loggins spent her final years
in Victoria, British Columbia, where
she enjoyed an active life.